"Meike Peters's new book is a soul-satisfying reminder that lunch is a state of mind. In our ever-busier lives, taking a break for a nourishing meal is the ultimate form of midday self-care. Having this repertoire of gorgeous, unfussy recipes—plus a smart set of tips, tricks, and strategies—only makes this proposition more delicious."

—ADEENA SUSSMAN, author of *Sababa*

"As someone who eschews breakfast and counts down the hours to lunch, *Noon* is right up my proverbial alley. Peters's recipes showcase the power of food to excite, to create a mood, or to transform a situation as much as to nourish the body. The joy of a midday feast is something within our reach with this beautiful book."

—HELEN GOH, coauthor of *Sweet*

"*Noon* has so many colorful, easy-to-make, and mouth-watering plates of food. I love the idea of midday feasting."

—SAMI TAMIMI, chef and award-winning author

"I have a feeling that I've been waiting for this exact book. Meike Peters manages to revive a time and a meal of the day that, due to our obsession with efficiency, we have almost forgotten about. And she does it in such a beautiful, practical, and original way that you want to drop everything and start cooking right away. I heartily recommend this book!"

—DANIEL SCHREIBER, author of *Susan Sontag*

NOON

NO

ON

Simple Recipes for Scrumptious
Midday Meals and More

Meike Peters

CHRONICLE BOOKS
SAN FRANCISCO

Library of Congress Cataloging-in-Publication Data available.

ISBN 978-1-7972-2280-6

Manufactured in China.

Editorial direction by Holly La Due.
Design by Vanessa Dina.
Prop styling by Meike Peters.
Food styling and photography by Meike Peters.
Author photograph by Anne Deppe.
Typesetting by Frank Brayton.

10 9 8 7 6 5 4 3 2 1

Chronicle books and gifts are available at special quantity discounts to corporations, professional associations, literacy programs, and other organizations. For details and discount information, please contact our premiums department at corporatesales@chroniclebooks.com or at 1-800-759-0190.

Chronicle Books LLC
680 Second Street
San Francisco, California 94107
www.chroniclebooks.com

For Anne, Toni, Gabi, and Laurel. To friendship.

Introduction

Breakfast never really excites me, but at noon, I feast. There's an old church opposite from where I live in Berlin, and as soon as the bells begin ringing twelve times, my stomach knows it's time to go to the kitchen and have fun. When I call it a feast, it doesn't mean that I cook for hours—it's the opposite. I learned that, with just a few tricks, I can indulge in the most satisfying meal at twelve o'clock, a meal that makes my mind, soul, and body happy. Lunchtime can easily be as exciting as dinner; we just need to keep our recipe choices realistic. Then it's pure joy to treat the palate to vibrant salads and vegetable dishes, to lush sandwiches, genius pastas, or warming soups. Even meat and seafood can easily make it onto our lunch table. It's just about the right choices and a bit of planning ahead.

So how do we get there? By reducing ingredients and focusing on bold, fresh flavors, skipping elaborate steps that don't fit into a busy schedule, and using pantry staples that save time. By relying on canned beans and lentils that don't require soaking and making a large jar of pesto to use for pasta, sandwiches, salads, and even soups. When roasting vegetables, throw a bunch on the baking sheet right from the start and use them for multiple recipes. Pasta dishes generally don't need many components, just a few good ingredients and clever combinations. A quiche, cold or warm, with its buttery short-crust base is bliss, especially at noon. Bake it in the evening or keep some pastry in the freezer for unexpected cravings.

When salads look and taste fresh and colorful, with layers of flavor and texture, it's fun for the eyes and the taste buds, but it's also nourishing. Take blood orange, radicchio, and mozzarella di bufala—or roasted squash, kale, and Stilton—toss them with a simple vinaigrette, dip a thick slice of bread into the juices, and you have a complete meal that puts a smile on your face. You will find many recipes in this book that you can prepare very spontaneously, working with what we usually find on our kitchen counter, on our pantry shelves, and in the fridge. And if you won't be home for lunch, most of the recipes can be prepared in advance, packed in containers, and assembled at work—hungry looks from your colleagues guaranteed. You can easily stuff leftover vegetables, but also schnitzel, tiny meatballs, or a slice of a Mediterranean meatloaf, into a ciabatta bun, and it's the best sandwich in the world. It often doesn't even matter whether you eat it cold or warm. If the flavors are balanced and the textures are satisfying, you can enjoy a dish right away or out of a lunch box at work.

Our idea of vegetable dishes changed tremendously in the past decade. Rather than seeing our daily greens as a side dish, veggies and legumes have become the centerpieces of recipes. Fresh herbs, fennel or coriander seeds, and citrus zest all add excitement. Trying unusual combinations that work well but also surprise and wake up our palate keeps noon tasty.

It's thrilling to come up with exuberant dinner plans to treat friends and family to—when they gather around my long wooden table, I have some of the happiest moments of my life—but at noon, I take a different approach. Rather than defining a meal, this book defines the time of the day when we all have our own preferences and focus on our own needs. Some go for light and fresh dishes, while others indulge in comfort food or crave the simple, honest pleasure of carbs. Sandwiches are the quickest solution for a satiating and lavish break. A bowl of oats topped with fruit is a hug for the soul, and so are pancakes, be they traditional German apple pancakes, a Breton galette, or pancakes topped with basil sugar.

But what we all have in common at noon is that we are looking for a meal that is nourishing, comforting, and healthy, a meal that gives us energy for the rest of the day and that is good for our body and soul. Instead of regularly searching for this outside of our kitchens and eating out, we can keep it in our own hands and increase the likelihood that we will find what we're actually looking for. Cooking and preparing our lunch at home, even in advance, doesn't need to be an impossible challenge.

Let's keep it realistic. Overwhelming our logistical skills doesn't help. What we need is an easy approach. So, the dishes in *Noon* are exciting yet simple and equally fitting to the start, the middle, or the end of our day. Double the amount of a minestrone recipe and you can have it one day for lunch, then add a poached egg or tiny meatballs for dinner the following evening. A colorful salad can herald the start of a day at breakfast just as much as closing it at dinnertime. Although this book is called *Noon*, the recipes work for the entire day, and both weekdays and weekends. Multiply the recipes and you can even turn them into starters and mains for relaxed dinner parties. *Noon* captures a feeling that recurs during the cycle of each day, a desire for a scrumptious break, for something uplifting, and for some time for ourselves and our own needs.

Good noon!

Notes on Kitchen Equipment and Ingredients

To keep it simple and not overcomplicate the kitchen, the tools I really need and enjoy the most are sharp knives—even just one—a large wooden cutting board, a small collection of stainless steel pots, and a heavy cast-iron skillet.

I use an electric stove, reliable but nothing fancy. The recipes in this book use conventional oven settings, as opposed to the broiler, unless specified. As every stove and oven work a little differently, the most important rule for the cook is: Stay attentive and watch, taste, and smell your food. When you build a connection to the dish you are cooking, it helps lead to the results you have in mind.

When you reduce the ingredients for a recipe, it's even more important that each one of them tastes good. If you go for quality produce and products, you will be more satisfied with your cooking.

The amount of food that each person enjoys varies, especially at noon. So, if you already know you want a bigger or smaller portion while you are chopping the vegetables, just double or halve the recipe.

The listed weight always indicates the amount after peeling, coring, and pitting. If not stated as peeled, vegetables and fruits are rinsed and scrubbed. Onions and garlic are peeled. If using citrus peel, the fruit should be organic, rinsed, and scrubbed. Meat and seafood are always briefly rinsed under cold water and dried with paper towels.

The pancake and tart recipes in this book call for all-purpose flour. I use all-purpose unbleached wheat flour or white spelt flour, which are similar in taste and texture (for both, 1 cup equals 4½ ounces / 130 g).

I only use olive oil in my kitchen, extra-virgin olive oil with deep flavor and color for salads and a mild one with a higher smoke point that is safe for cooking. There are two vinegars on my kitchen shelf, a dark balsamic vinegar and a white balsamic vinegar. I use Mediterranean flaky sea salt (whole flakes or finely ground with a mortar and pestle) and black peppercorns. Spices are mostly used whole, then crushed with a mortar and pestle. Although I love to indulge in a variety of fresh herbs, for *Noon*, I keep it simple and use what flourishes on a windowsill or city balcony, such as basil, rosemary, and thyme.

SALADS

Radicchio with Blood Orange and Mozzarella di Bufala

SERVES 2

FOR THE SALAD

4 large radicchio leaves, torn into pieces

1 large Belgian endive, thickly cut crosswise

2 small blood oranges, peeled (skin and white pith removed) and cut into thick slices

4 ounces (110 g) mozzarella di bufala, drained and torn into chunky pieces

1 small handful fresh basil leaves

FOR THE DRESSING

3 tablespoons olive oil

2 tablespoons white balsamic vinegar

Fine sea salt

Coarsely ground pepper

Sweet and sour, bitter, juicy, and creamy—the flavors and textures in this salad pop on your tongue and the colors brighten up even the gloomiest day. Food is flavor, but it's also fun. Just like music, it can deepen the mood we're in, as well as bring us into a different frame of mind. A meal has the power to make us smile, make our body and mind feel good, and give our soul the tender hug it needs. This salad will squeeze your weary soul with verve and relax you—even during a busy schedule. It's a quick dish but pure joy to eat.

For the salad, arrange the radicchio, Belgian endive, blood orange, mozzarella, and basil on individual plates.

For the dressing, whisk together the olive oil and vinegar in a small bowl, then season to taste with salt and pepper. Drizzle the dressing over the salad and enjoy immediately.

If you want to take the salad to work for your lunch break, pack the blood oranges at the bottom of a container, followed by the mozzarella, radicchio, endive, and basil. Keep the dressing in a separate jar and assemble just before eating.

Autumn Salad with Jerusalem Artichokes, Walnuts, and Apples

SERVES 2

FOR THE SALAD

Olive oil, for sautéing

5 ounces (140 g) peeled Jerusalem artichokes (or parsnip), cut into ¼-inch-thick (0.5 cm) round slices

Fine sea salt

Finely ground pepper

2 small Belgian endives

2 small, firm apples, cored and cut into quarters

1 small handful walnuts, roughly chopped

Flaky sea salt

FOR THE DRESSING

3 tablespoons olive oil

2 tablespoons white balsamic vinegar

Fine sea salt

Finely ground pepper

Jerusalem artichoke (sunchoke) is a vegetable I often forget about. The lumpy tuber, which is not an artichoke and actually a variety of sunflower, camouflages well in the vegetable section. But every once in a while, I remind myself of its sweet, nutty taste, and use it to cozy up autumn and winter salads. Sautéed for just a few minutes, then snuggled up to Belgian endive, apples, and walnuts, it becomes a salad that is nourishing and feels like a proper meal. If you can't find knobby Jerusalem artichoke, there's no need to skip this recipe—simply replace it with parsnip. Its sweetness comes with a little spice, which is nice; it just needs to cook a little longer.

For the salad, heat a splash of olive oil in a medium, heavy pan over medium-high heat. Add the Jerusalem artichokes, arranging them next to each other, and sauté, stirring and turning them occasionally, for about 5 minutes or until golden brown and tender. Season to taste with fine sea salt and pepper and set aside.

Cut 1 Belgian endive crosswise and separate the whole leaves of the second Belgian endive, then transfer both to a large plate. Arrange the apples and sautéed Jerusalem artichokes on top and sprinkle with the walnuts and a little flaky sea salt.

For the dressing, whisk together the olive oil and vinegar in a small bowl and season to taste with fine sea salt and pepper. Drizzle the dressing over the salad and enjoy.

If you want to take the salad to work, pack the cooled Jerusalem artichokes at the bottom of a container, then layer the Belgian endives, apples, and walnuts on top. Keep the dressing in a separate jar and assemble just before your lunch break.

Potato and Green Bean Salad with Asparagus and Poached Eggs

SERVES 2

FOR THE SALAD

6 ounces (170 g) trimmed romano beans (or green beans)

4 ounces (110 g) trimmed green asparagus

10 ounces (280 g) small waxy potatoes, boiled and cut in half

2 large eggs, poached (page 115)

1 small handful sliced ramp leaves or scallions (green part only)

FOR THE DRESSING

3 tablespoons olive oil

2 tablespoons white balsamic vinegar

1 teaspoon Dijon mustard, plus more to taste

Fine sea salt

Coarsely ground pepper

I love a hearty German potato salad all year round, but adding blanched green beans and asparagus and crowning it with a poached egg makes it fit for spring. Sprinkled with sliced ramp leaves or scallions, it smells, looks, and tastes as fresh as a walk through the woods. The dressing, a simple vinaigrette refined with Dijon mustard, is a little peppery in the nose and wakes you up—just as spring does. You can use regular green beans, but if you find flat romano beans at the farmers' market, try these— they are perfect for potato salad.

For the salad, bring a large pot of salted water to a boil and blanch the beans for about 5 minutes or until tender. Leave the pot on the heat and, using a slotted ladle or spoon, transfer the beans to a colander. Drain and briefly rinse the beans with cold water, then transfer to a cutting board. Add the asparagus to the boiling water and blanch for 3 minutes or until al dente. Drain and briefly rinse the asparagus with cold water, then place on the cutting board. Cut the asparagus and beans into bite-size pieces.

For the dressing, whisk together the olive oil, vinegar, and mustard in a small bowl and season to taste with salt, pepper, and additional mustard.

Layer the potatoes, beans, and asparagus on a large platter or plate and drizzle with the dressing; you might have to add a little more salt and pepper to the vegetables. Arrange the poached eggs on top of the vegetables, sprinkle with the ramp leaves, and enjoy.

If you want to take the salad to work, pack the cooled vegetables and ramp leaves in a container and keep the dressing separate in a jar. Replace the poached eggs with hard-boiled eggs, place them on top of the vegetables, and assemble the salad just before your lunch break.

Cucumber and Fennel Salad with Melon

SERVES 1

½ small fennel bulb, cored and thinly sliced lengthwise

⅓ large cucumber, scrubbed and cut into cubes

1 wedge ripe melon (cantaloupe, honeydew, or Galia), peeled and thickly sliced crosswise

1½ tablespoons olive oil

1 tablespoon freshly squeezed lemon juice

¼ teaspoon fennel seeds (or aniseeds), ground with a mortar and pestle, plus a few seeds for serving

Fine sea salt

Finely ground pepper

Flaky sea salt

For a garden party at my mother's house, a friend drowned chunks of soft cantaloupe in pastis, the anise-flavored French apéritif. It became a strong flavor memory that I often go back to. Combined in a dish, ripe fruit and anise taste like Mediterranean summer: warm and sweet, pure and raw. Fennel bulb and cucumber are both crisp and fresh, perfect to complement juicy, ripe melon. The dressing, made of olive oil, lemon juice, salt, and pepper, is refined with freshly ground fennel seeds or aniseeds—this way you can skip the boozy pastis.

Layer the fennel, cucumber, and melon on a plate.

In a small bowl, whisk together the olive oil, lemon juice, and ground fennel seeds. Season to taste with fine sea salt and pepper, then drizzle over the salad. Sprinkle the salad with a few whole fennel seeds and a little flaky sea salt and enjoy.

To prepare the salad to take to work, pack the vegetables and fruit together in a container and keep the dressing separate in a jar; assemble just before your lunch break.

Crisped Chickpeas with Belgian Endive and Strawberries

SERVES 2

FOR THE SALAD

Olive oil, for searing

1¼ cups (250 g) drained and rinsed canned chickpeas

2 tablespoons freshly squeezed orange juice

Fine sea salt

Finely ground pepper

½ medium yellow Belgian endive, whole leaves separated

½ medium red Belgian endive, whole leaves separated

5 large strawberries, hulled and cut in half lengthwise

1 small handful fresh basil leaves

FOR THE DRESSING

2 tablespoons olive oil

2 tablespoons freshly squeezed orange juice

Fine sea salt

Finely ground pepper

Crisped chickpeas love strawberries. And basil. Toss this velvety, sweet salad with a light orange vinaigrette, and it will make everyone happy. Add some whole Belgian endive leaves—you can use red and yellow leaves to enhance the visual drama—and you have even more contrast in taste and texture. Endive is crisp, a bit bitter, and also practical: You can use the leaves to scoop up the chickpeas.

For the salad, heat a splash of olive oil in a large, heavy pan over high heat. Add the chickpeas, cover (they will pop), and sear, stirring and shaking the pan, for 2 to 3 minutes or until golden and crispy; mind that they don't burn and reduce the heat if necessary. Transfer the chickpeas to a medium bowl, stir in the orange juice, and season to taste with salt and pepper; let them cool for a few minutes.

For the dressing, whisk together the olive oil and orange juice in a small bowl and season to taste with salt and pepper.

Layer the yellow and red Belgian endive leaves, chickpeas, and strawberries on a large plate or platter. Drizzle with the dressing, sprinkle with the basil, and enjoy.

To transport the salad to work, pack the Belgian endives, cooled chickpeas, strawberries, and basil in a container and keep the dressing separate in a jar; assemble just before lunch.

Artichokes, Butter Beans, and Pink Grapefruit with Pistachios

SERVES 2

FOR THE SALAD

1¼ cups (250 g) drained and rinsed canned butter beans (lima beans)

2 large artichoke hearts, marinated in olive oil, each cut into 6 wedges

1 pink grapefruit or orange (or 2 tangerines), peeled (skin and white pith removed) and cut into segments

1 small handful salted pistachios, roughly chopped

Flaky sea salt

FOR THE DRESSING

3 tablespoons olive oil

2 tablespoons freshly squeezed lemon juice

Fine sea salt

Finely ground pepper

Marinated artichoke hearts, grapefruit, and salty pistachios is a combination charged with excitement—and makes for a speedy salad if you're in the mood for something refreshing. The artichoke hearts can be store-bought, either from a jar or the deli counter. Cutting away the pith from the citrus fruit's slender segments is the part that takes the longest, but to save time, you can just peel it and cut thick slices. Orange or tangerine fits in as well, replacing the grapefruit's bitter note with subtle sweetness.

For the salad, layer the butter beans, artichoke hearts, and grapefruit on a large, deep plate.

For the dressing, whisk together the olive oil and lemon juice in a small bowl and season to taste with fine sea salt and pepper. Drizzle the dressing over the salad and sprinkle with the pistachios and a little flaky sea salt. Enjoy the salad immediately or within 1 to 2 hours.

If you want to take the salad to work, you can combine everything a couple of hours in advance and pack it in a lunch box, but store the pistachios separately and add them later; otherwise, they will lose their crunch.

Lemony Fennel, Persimmon, and Burrata

SERVES 2

FOR THE SALAD

10 ounces (280 g) cored fennel bulb, thinly sliced lengthwise, plus a few chopped fronds

1 large ripe persimmon, peeled and cut into wedges

4 ounces (110 g) burrata or mozzarella di bufala, drained and torn in half

1 to 2 teaspoons freshly grated lemon zest

FOR THE DRESSING

3 tablespoons olive oil

1 tablespoon white balsamic vinegar

1 tablespoon freshly squeezed lemon juice

Fine sea salt

Coarsely ground pepper

Creamy burrata, sprinkled with good olive oil and freshly grated lemon zest, is simply divine. It looks and tastes tempting and lush, and it's the quickest lunch. You just need to stick to quality ingredients. Since I had this at a dinner in Rome, it's become a recurring treat when I need to remind myself that every day can be a feast—at least in the kitchen. A bed of thin fennel slices and ripe persimmon, sweet like honey, enhances the pleasure. Although it may not seem like it, this can be easily prepared in advance, packed separately, and assembled at work. How luxurious is that?

For the salad, divide the sliced fennel between two plates, arrange the persimmon and burrata on top, then sprinkle with the fennel fronds and the lemon zest.

For the dressing, whisk together the olive oil, vinegar, and lemon juice in a small bowl and season to taste with salt and pepper. Drizzle the dressing over the salad and serve immediately.

To prepare the salad for work, pack the sliced fennel at the bottom of a container, followed by the persimmon, burrata, fennel fronds, and lemon zest, but keep the dressing separate in a jar; assemble just before lunch.

Roasted Squash, Parsnip, and Grape Salad with Blue Cheese

SERVES 2

FOR THE SALAD

12 ounces (340 g) seeded squash, preferably peeled butternut or Hokkaido with skin, cut into 1-inch (2.5 cm) wedges

6 ounces (170 g) seedless red grapes, on the vine

3 ounces (85 g) peeled parsnip, cut into wedges

¼ cup (60 ml) olive oil

Flaky sea salt

6 large radicchio leaves, torn into large pieces

8 small romaine lettuce leaves

1½ ounces (40 g) Roquefort or Stilton, crumbled (optional)

FOR THE DRESSING

3 tablespoons olive oil

2 tablespoons white balsamic vinegar

Fine sea salt

Finely ground pepper

In this salad, autumn is at last as bright and vibrant as the previous season. Parsnip, squash, and grapes, all roasted on one baking sheet, are layered with fresh green lettuce and radicchio leaves. A quick vinaigrette and a handful of blue cheese crumbled on top—just for fun—round it out. This is the perfect salad for a day when you don't mind turning on your oven and can let the veggies roast for thirty minutes while you do a bit more work at your desk or just relax. You can roast everything in advance and double the recipe to use leftovers for other salads (pages 31 and 53), sandwiches (page 152), or soups (page 125).

Preheat the oven to 400°F (200°C).

For the salad, spread the squash, grapes, and parsnip on a large baking sheet, but keep them separate. Drizzle with the olive oil and gently toss to coat, again keeping the squash, grapes, and parsnip separate. Season with a little flaky sea salt and roast for 15 minutes, then gently flip the squash and parsnip over and continue roasting for 10 to 15 minutes or until the squash and parsnip are tender and the grapes start to soften. Remove from the oven and let everything cool on the baking sheet for 5 minutes.

For the dressing, whisk together the olive oil and vinegar in a small bowl and season to taste with fine sea salt and pepper.

Divide the radicchio and lettuce leaves between two large plates and layer the squash, parsnip, and grapes (on the vine or snipped) on top. Sprinkle with the Roquefort, drizzle with the dressing, and serve immediately.

To prepare the salad for transportation, let the squash, parsnip, and grapes (off the vine) cool completely, then pack in a container and spread the radicchio, lettuce leaves, and Roquefort on top. Keep the dressing separate in a jar and assemble just before lunch.

Autumn Panzanella with Roasted Squash, Shallots, and Plums

SERVES 2

FOR THE SALAD

11 ounces (310 g) seeded squash, preferably peeled butternut or Hokkaido with skin, cut into 1–inch (2.5 cm) wedges

1 tablespoon olive oil

Flaky sea salt

4 shallots, unpeeled

1 medium red or yellow Belgian endive, trimmed and leaves separated

2 large dark plums, each cut into 8 wedges

2 handfuls chunky dark spelt or rye bread cubes

2 tablespoons pumpkin seeds

1 ounce (30 g) Stilton or Roquefort, crumbled (optional)

FOR THE DRESSING

3 tablespoons olive oil

2 tablespoons balsamic vinegar

Fine sea salt

Finely ground pepper

Panzanella easily adapts to your mood, your appetite, and the seasons. It can be light and simple or rich and nourishing. If a Greek salad tossed with chunky cubes of white bread screams "summer" (page 33), this version, catching the tail end of stone fruits, gently whispers "autumn." It's cozy and comforting. Roasted squash and shallots welcome dark plums, red Belgian endive, pumpkin seeds, and Stilton. You could leave out the cheese, but then you'd miss out on the sharp punch that it adds. To complement the complex flavors in this recipe, I go for dark spelt or rye bread. It's heartier and has more depth.

Preheat the oven to 400°F (200°C).

For the salad, spread the squash in a large baking dish, toss with the olive oil, and season with a little flaky sea salt. Add the shallots and roast for 15 minutes, then gently flip the squash and continue roasting for 10 to 15 minutes or until the squash is tender. Remove from the oven and let everything cool for 5 minutes. Cut the squash wedges in half crosswise, then cut the ends off the shallots, peel them, and cut them in half lengthwise.

For the dressing, whisk together the olive oil and vinegar in a small bowl and season to taste with fine sea salt and pepper.

Layer the Belgian endive leaves, plums, squash, shallots, and bread cubes in two medium bowls. Sprinkle with the pumpkin seeds and Stilton, drizzle with the dressing, and enjoy.

If packing the salad for work, store the vegetables and fruit in a container and spread the bread cubes, pumpkin seeds, and cheese on top. Keep the dressing separate in a jar until ready to eat.

Greek Panzanella

SERVES 2

FOR THE SALAD

1 large, thick slice white sourdough bread with crust (about 4 ounces / 110 g), cut into cubes

1 large tomato, cut into wedges

1 Persian cucumber (about 4 ounces / 110 g), scrubbed, cut in half lengthwise, and cut into thick slices

½ yellow bell pepper, cut into thin slices

4 ounces (110 g) feta, broken into small chunks

6 large Kalamata olives

1 small handful fresh mint leaves (optional)

FOR THE DRESSING

3 tablespoons olive oil

1 tablespoon balsamic vinegar

1 tablespoon freshly squeezed lemon juice

Fine sea salt

Finely ground pepper

Imagine a Greek salad, crisp and colorful, with ripe tomatoes, juicy cucumber, sweet bell pepper, and salty feta. Now imagine a Tuscan bread salad, the famous panzanella. It uses almost the same ingredients as the salad from Greece, but instead of feta there are chunky cubes of white bread. Now combine these two dishes in your mind and you'll have an idea of this Greek Panzanella. When the temperature goes up and the sun is straight above your head, there's no better lunch you can place on the table. It's light and fresh and won't leave you hungry—it's also a fantastic side dish for pan- or oven-roasted fish, such as tuna or salmon (page 218).

For the salad, layer the bread cubes, tomato, cucumber, bell pepper, feta, and olives on a large plate or platter.

For the dressing, whisk together the olive oil, vinegar, and lemon juice in a small bowl and season to taste with salt and pepper. Drizzle the dressing over the salad and sprinkle with the mint leaves. Enjoy!

If taking the panzanella to work, pack the salad in a container, but keep the dressing separate in a jar and dress right before eating.

Carrot and Pear Salad with Tahini and Sesame Seeds

SERVES 1

1 teaspoon white
sesame seeds

1 tablespoon light tahini

1 tablespoon water

Fine sea salt

2 medium carrots, peeled
and cut into thick slices

½ to 1 ripe pear, cored and
cut into wedges

1 teaspoon olive oil

Flaky sea salt

Coarsely ground pepper

When a friend pointed out that pear and sesame are a marvelous duo, my mind started spinning. Instead of trying to be too clever, I reminded myself that simplicity often works best when the combination is just right. Chunky raw carrot, slender pear wedges, a nutty tahini drizzle, toasted sesame seeds, and flaky sea salt are enough. They complement each other so smoothly that any further addition would only distract.

Heat a medium, heavy pan over medium-high heat without adding any fat. Add the sesame seeds to the hot pan and toast, stirring once, for 20 to 30 seconds or until fragrant; set the pan aside.

In a small bowl, whisk together the tahini, water, and a pinch of fine sea salt until smooth.

Arrange the carrots and pear on a plate and drizzle with the olive oil and the tahini dressing; you might not need all of the dressing. Sprinkle with the toasted sesame seeds, a little flaky sea salt, and pepper. Enjoy!

If you want to take the salad to work, pack the carrots and pear in a container, drizzle with the olive oil, and season with a little salt and pepper. Pack the tahini dressing and sesame seeds separately and assemble just before you want to eat.

Peach and Plum Caprese with Burrata

SERVES 1

FOR THE DRESSING

1½ tablespoons olive oil

1 tablespoon balsamic vinegar

Fine sea salt

Finely ground pepper

FOR THE SALAD

4 ounces (110 g) burrata
(or mozzarella di bufala),
torn in half

1 large peach, cut into
thin wedges

1 large dark plum, cut
into thin wedges

1 small handful fresh
basil leaves

A caprese salad is the essence of summer, and the essence of the Italian way of lunching: easy and relaxed, never forgetting that life is sweet. It's ideally enjoyed al fresco—a slice of fresh ciabatta squeezed between your fingers to soak up the sweet and tart juices on your plate—and maybe with a glass of crisp white wine if you're in the mood. The classic version is made with tomatoes, mozzarella, and basil, and drizzled with a dark vinaigrette. It's unbeatable and there's no need for another recipe. You just throw everything together with verve and gusto. However, when summer is coming to an end and I've already indulged in the familiar version many times, I like to replace the usual tomatoes with ripe peaches and firm plums. This caprese salad celebrates the quiet transition to early autumn, from lighter to heartier flavors, and from bright to dimmed colors.

For the dressing, whisk together the olive oil and vinegar in a small bowl and season to taste with salt and pepper.

For the salad, place the burrata in the middle of a plate and arrange the peach and plum wedges around it. Drizzle with the dressing, sprinkle with the basil, and enjoy.

To prepare the caprese for work, pack the peach and plum at the bottom of a container, followed by the burrata and basil. Keep the dressing separate in a jar and assemble just before your lunch break.

Chickpeas and Pear with Juniper and Hazelnuts

SERVES 1

4 medium juniper berries*

Fine sea salt

1 tablespoon olive oil

1 tablespoon freshly
squeezed lemon juice,
plus more to taste

⅔ cup (120 g) drained and
rinsed canned chickpeas

Finely ground pepper

¼ large, tender pear, cored
and cut into slices crosswise

10 hazelnuts, roughly
chopped

Here's a flavor experiment to surprise—or challenge—the palate. Nutty chickpeas, tender pear, crunchy hazelnuts, and a juniper-lemon vinaigrette sounds unusual, but it all mingles harmoniously. Juniper berries—sadly, not as widely known as they should be but still easy to find in the spice section of most grocery stores—bring in an unexpected flavor that easily charms anything nutty, as well as ripe fruit. The spice is potent but polite, pungent yet pleasant. Sometimes a small addition can change a whole composition. Four plump dark berries— they are actually cones and not true berries—turn a very simple salad into a more complex dish. I can't help but think of southern France, coastal pinewoods, and citrus when I eat it.

Using a mortar and pestle, pound and grind the juniper berries and ⅛ teaspoon of salt until fine and combined.

In a medium bowl, whisk together the olive oil, lemon juice, and the juniper-salt mixture, then add the chickpeas and toss to combine. Season to taste with salt, pepper, and additional lemon juice, then gently fold in the pear. Sprinkle with the hazelnuts and enjoy.

If you want to take the salad to work, toss the chickpeas and pear with the dressing, then transfer to a container. Keep the hazelnuts separate and assemble just before you want to eat.

* You could substitute the juniper berries with ¼ teaspoon of gin, but that will also make the salad boozy. Alternatively, leave out the juniper—the salad will still taste great, just a bit less special.

Tuscan Mixed Salad with Boiled Eggs and Tuna

FOR THE DRESSING

3 tablespoons olive oil

2 tablespoons balsamic vinegar

Fine sea salt

Finely ground pepper

FOR THE SALAD

1 small red Belgian endive, trimmed and leaves separated

½ head red leaf lettuce (like red oak leaf lettuce), trimmed and leaves separated

3 large radicchio leaves

4 radishes, cut in half

4 grape or cherry tomatoes, cut in half

½ red bell pepper, cut into cubes

3 ounces (85 g) drained canned tuna in water

2 hard-boiled large eggs, cut in half

1 medium carrot, coarsely grated

This is my go-to salad when I crave a huge plate full of tasty, vitamin-rich ingredients. Over the years I've come up with multiple variations, but during a Tuscan holiday at an old villa outside Lucca, I was presented with a colorful bowl that included a novelty. Along with the lettuce leaves, tomatoes, and bell peppers, the boiled eggs and canned tuna, were coarsely grated carrots. They add sweetness and beautifully blend into this vibrant, mostly red-hued recipe. Radicchio and red Belgian endive take care of the bitter tones, radishes make it a bit peppery, and tomatoes keep it juicy. It's a busy plate and flamboyant, yet it only features very basic produce. Feel free to follow your mood and turn it into a green salad—think of beans and peas—or go for yellow and let corn, yellow pepper, and golden tomatoes make an appearance. I prefer to keep the lettuce leaves whole, as they enhance the visual drama, and they won't soften as quickly.

For the dressing, whisk together the olive oil and vinegar in a small bowl and season to taste with salt and pepper.

For the salad, on a large plate or platter, layer the Belgian endive leaves, lettuce, radicchio leaves, radishes, tomatoes, and bell pepper. Place the tuna and eggs in the middle. Sprinkle with the carrot, drizzle with the dressing, and enjoy!

If you want to prepare the salad in advance, layer all the vegetables in a container and place the eggs on top. Keep the tuna in the can and the dressing separate in a jar and arrange the salad just before you want to eat it.

Cilantro, Beet, and Grape Salad

SERVES 1

FOR THE SALAD

1 medium beet, scrubbed

1 large bay leaf

1 large handful fresh cilantro stalks and leaves

1 small handful seedless red grapes

FOR THE DRESSING

1 tablespoon olive oil

2 teaspoons balsamic vinegar

Fine sea salt

Finely ground pepper

During a trip to Japan, I tried a stunningly simple salad made with fresh cilantro, using both the leaves and the stalks. I was smitten. I was introduced to it at an izakaya in Tokyo, during a late, jet-lagged night filled with ecstatic restaurant hopping. The salad was drizzled only with olive oil and lemon juice and tossed with very thinly sliced red onion. As soon as I got home, I started playing with it. Earthy beet and plump red grapes work extremely well with the distinct taste of this delicate herb. You should use the cilantro generously in this quick salad, thinking of it as a lettuce and not as an herb.

For the salad, bring a small pot of salted water to a boil. Add the beet and bay leaf, then reduce the heat, cover, and simmer for 45 to 50 minutes or until the beet is tender. Drain the beet and quickly rinse with cold water. Let the beet cool completely, then peel and cut into wedges.

Arrange the cilantro, beet, and grapes on a plate.

For the dressing, whisk together the olive oil and vinegar in a small bowl and season to taste with salt and pepper. Drizzle the dressing over the salad, toss, and enjoy immediately.

If you want to take the salad to work, pack the cilantro, beet, and grapes in a container. Keep the dressing separate in a jar and assemble just before you want to eat it.

Red Cabbage and Beet Salad
with Persimmon and Stilton

SERVES 2

FOR THE SALAD

1 large beet, scrubbed

1 bay leaf

Fine sea salt

10 ounces (280 g) cored
red cabbage, shredded

1 large ripe Hachiya
persimmon, peeled and cut
into wedges

2 ounces (60 g) Stilton or
Roquefort, crumbled

2 teaspoons fresh thyme
leaves

Coarsely ground pepper

FOR THE DRESSING

3 tablespoons olive oil

1 tablespoon balsamic vinegar

1 tablespoon white
balsamic vinegar

½ teaspoon honey

Fine sea salt

Finely ground pepper

It took me years to use red cabbage in salads. In my mind, the purple head was reserved for sweet and sour Rotkohl, cooked with red wine and warming spices for Weihnachten, German Christmas Eve. Although I got used to the idea of making a raw red cabbage salad, I still like to stick to sweet and sour and throw in other strong flavors to mingle with the peppery leaves. Persimmon—the riper and softer the better—beet wedges, and blue cheese happily join in, tossed with a dark vinaigrette and sweetened with honey. You can easily prepare the components of this salad in advance, double the recipe, and enjoy it over the course of a few days. I always cook a bunch of beets right away and use them for various salads (page 43) or just drizzle them with olive oil and sprinkle them with sea salt for an unbeatable snack.

For the salad, bring a medium pot of salted water to a boil. Add the beet and bay leaf, then reduce the heat, cover, and simmer for 45 to 50 minutes or until the beet is tender. Drain the beet and quickly rinse with cold water. Let the beet cool completely, then peel and cut into wedges.

In a large bowl, sprinkle ¾ teaspoon of salt over the cabbage, rub it in with your fingers for about 1 minute, and let it sit for 10 minutes to soften.

For the dressing, whisk together the olive oil, balsamic and white balsamic vinegars, and honey in a small bowl and season with a little salt and pepper; mind that the cabbage is already salted.

Divide the cabbage, beet, and persimmon between two plates and arrange the Stilton on top. Drizzle with the dressing, sprinkle with the thyme and a little coarsely ground pepper, and enjoy.

To prepare the salad for work, pack the vegetables, fruit, and Stilton in a container and sprinkle with the thyme; you can skip the coarsely ground pepper. Keep the dressing separate in a jar and dress right before eating.

Asparagus, Green Bean, and Pea Salad
with Peach and Chèvre

SERVES 2

FOR THE SALAD

7 ounces (200 g) trimmed green asparagus

6 ounces (170 g) trimmed romano beans or green beans

4 ounces (110 g) fresh or frozen peas

1 large peach, cut into 8 wedges

2 ounces (60 g) aged chèvre, cut into thin slices

FOR THE DRESSING

3 tablespoons olive oil

2 tablespoons white balsamic vinegar

1 small bunch fresh dill, trimmed and fronds finely chopped

Fine sea salt

Coarsely ground pepper

Sometimes it's the thrilling play of flavors that excites us about a dish; other times it's contrasting textures. Visual harmony can be just as enticing. Here, we concentrate on green vegetables, all a little sweet and very fresh. Green asparagus, beans, and peas unite on a platter to welcome mature chèvre and lush, juicy peach. The fruit enhances the natural sweetness of the veggies, while the cheese introduces a tart note. The green vinaigrette, thickened with lots of fresh dill, resembles pesto more than dressing. It's all very vibrant and light, plus packed with lots of vitamins.

For the salad, bring a large pot of salted water to a boil and blanch the asparagus for about 3 minutes or until al dente. Leave the pot on the heat and, using a slotted ladle or spoon, transfer the asparagus to a colander. Briefly rinse the asparagus with cold water, then transfer to a cutting board. Add the beans to the boiling water and blanch for 5 minutes or until tender. Add the peas and continue cooking for 1 minute. Drain and briefly rinse the beans and peas with cold water. Transfer the beans to the cutting board and the peas to a bowl, then cut the asparagus and beans into bite-size pieces.

For the dressing, whisk together the olive oil, vinegar, and dill in a small bowl and season to taste with salt and pepper.

Layer the asparagus, beans, peas, peach, and chèvre on a large platter or plate and drizzle with the dressing; you might have to add a little more salt and pepper to the vegetables. Enjoy immediately.

If taking the salad to work, pack the cooled vegetables in a container and place the fruit and cheese on top. Keep the dressing separate in a jar and dress right before eating.

Fennel Carpaccio with Balsamic Seared Plums

SERVES 1

1 tablespoon olive oil, plus
more for searing

2 large dark plums, pitted
and cut into quarters

1 teaspoon balsamic vinegar

1 small fennel bulb, cored and
thinly sliced lengthwise, plus
a few chopped fronds

1½ teaspoons freshly
squeezed lemon juice

Fine sea salt

Coarsely ground pepper

Flaky sea salt

This salad is a confident stunner. Although the ingredient list is short, the results are spectacular. Raw fennel, thinly sliced like carpaccio and licoricey sweet like aniseed, delivers a strong contrast to dark plums cooked in balsamic. Briefly seared in a hot pan, the stone fruits are sour and tender but not soft, still holding their shape. You could crumble mature Stilton or Roquefort over the duo, adding another layer of flavor and more complexity. It would totally make sense, but I got so excited by the simplicity of this recipe that I decided: No cheese for me this time.

In a medium, heavy pan, heat a small splash of olive oil over medium-high heat. Add the plums and sear for 1½ to 2 minutes on each cut side or until golden brown but not dark; mind that they still hold their shape. Add the vinegar, stir, and cook for 10 seconds, then take the pan off the heat and set aside.

Layer the sliced fennel on a plate and arrange the plums on top.

Whisk together the 1 tablespoon of olive oil and the lemon juice in a small bowl and season to taste with fine sea salt and pepper. Drizzle the dressing over the salad and sprinkle with the fennel fronds and a little flaky sea salt. Enjoy immediately.

To prepare the salad for work, pack the sliced fennel in a container and place the plums and fennel fronds on top, but skip the flaky sea salt. Keep the dressing separate in a jar and dress just before your lunch break.

Seared Zucchini and Chickpea Salad with Grapes

SERVES 1

FOR THE SALAD

Olive oil, for searing

½ medium zucchini, cut into ⅓-inch-thick (0.75 cm) round slices

Fine sea salt

Finely ground pepper

⅔ cup (120 g) drained and rinsed canned chickpeas

1 handful arugula leaves

1 small handful seedless red grapes

FOR THE DRESSING

2 tablespoons olive oil

2 tablespoons freshly squeezed orange juice

Fine sea salt

Finely ground pepper

Seared zucchini is one of the most versatile and reliable—but also underrated—additions to quick salads and pasta dishes. That's why I always keep at least one in the fridge. Although its peak season is in summer, you can get quality zucchini all year round. Whether I cut it into thick or slender slices, I always cook zucchini briefly over high heat, keeping it at the edge of firm to tender. This way it stays juicy. One of zucchini's most charming qualities is that it never tries to dominate a dish; it finds its place but doesn't vanish either. Its sweet side goes well with canned chickpeas, fresh grapes, and arugula leaves, or any other green lettuce you have lying around in your fridge. You just need to drizzle it with an orange vinaigrette for a quick and comforting lunch salad.

For the salad, heat a splash of olive oil in a small, heavy pan over medium-high heat. Add the zucchini and sear, turning once, for 1 to 2 minutes per side or until golden and just tender. Season to taste with salt and pepper, transfer to a plate, and take the pan off the heat. Add the chickpeas to the pan, season with a little salt and pepper, stir, and set aside.

For the dressing, whisk together the olive oil and orange juice in a small bowl and season to taste with salt and pepper.

Layer the arugula, chickpeas, zucchini, and grapes in a little bowl and drizzle with the dressing; enjoy.

If you want to take the salad to work, pack the cooled zucchini and chickpeas in a container and place the grapes and arugula on top. Keep the dressing separate in a jar and assemble just before you want to eat.

Lentil Salad with Roasted Squash and Lemon

SERVES 2

FOR THE SQUASH

12 ounces (340 g) seeded squash, preferably peeled butternut or Hokkaido with skin, cut into 1-inch (2.5 cm) wedges

2 tablespoons olive oil

Flaky sea salt

FOR THE SALAD

⅔ cup (140 g) small, green or French Puy lentils (no soaking required)

6 sprigs fresh thyme

2 small bay leaves

1 tablespoon olive oil

1 to 2 tablespoons freshly squeezed lemon juice

Fine sea salt

Finely ground pepper

1 handful arugula leaves

2 to 3 teaspoons freshly grated lemon zest

Lentils are nutty and nourishing, and always manage to create a feeling of comfort. Even in a cold salad, they spread an aura of coziness. They are the kind of food you want to eat when you need a little break from the world. Topping dark green Puy lentils with roasted squash wedges is particularly satisfying. The squash can be roasted a day ahead, as it doesn't need to be warm, and the salad can sit for a few hours, but you should add the arugula just before serving. You can also double the recipe and use cold leftover squash for other salads (pages 28 and 31) or a sandwich (page 152).

Preheat the oven to 400°F (200°C).

For the squash, spread the squash in a large baking dish, drizzle with the olive oil, and toss to coat, then season with a little flaky sea salt. Roast the squash for 15 minutes, gently flip the wedges over, and continue roasting for 10 to 15 minutes or until tender.

For the salad, while the squash is roasting, place the lentils in a medium saucepan with plenty of (unsalted) water, add the thyme and bay leaves, and bring to a boil. Reduce the heat and simmer, adding more water, if necessary, for about 20 minutes or until al dente (or follow the package instructions). Remove and discard the herbs, then drain the lentils in a sieve for at least 5 minutes.

Transfer the lentils to a medium bowl and stir in the olive oil and 1 tablespoon of the lemon juice, adding more lemon juice to taste. Season to taste with fine sea salt and pepper and divide between two bowls, layering the lentils with the arugula. Arrange the roasted squash on top and generously sprinkle with lemon zest. Enjoy!

If taking the salad to work, assemble and pack the salad without the arugula in a container. Keep the arugula separate, folding it in right before eating.

Krautsalat with Dates and Bacon

SERVES 2

Fine sea salt

8 ounces (225 g) cored green cabbage, shredded

Olive oil, for cooking

2 ounces (60 g) thick-cut bacon, cut into very small cubes

1½ tablespoons white balsamic vinegar

2 large, juicy dates, cut in half, pitted, and cut into thin strips lengthwise

Finely ground pepper

German Krautsalat, or coleslaw, is a quick and nourishing lunch—and dinner—option. You start by rubbing shredded green cabbage with a little salt, letting it sit for ten minutes to soften the leaves, and then you can play around. The good thing about coleslaw is that you don't have to worry about knocking the raw cabbage out with other ingredients; it can deal with bold companions. Sweet and salty goes very well with it, so tender dates and crunchy bacon are an ideal pairing. The bacon is deglazed with white balsamic vinegar, turning the meaty pan juices into a silky dressing. I strongly recommend using very good, soft, and juicy large dates, such as Medjool. Don't even bother using hard, dried-out fruit; it will only make this salad—and you—unhappy.

In a large bowl, sprinkle ½ teaspoon of salt over the cabbage, rub it in with your fingers for about 1 minute, and let it sit for 10 minutes to soften.

In a medium, heavy pan, heat a tiny splash of olive oil over medium-high heat. Add the bacon and cook, reducing the heat, if necessary, for about 8 minutes or until golden brown and very crispy. Deglaze the pan with the vinegar, using a spatula to scrape any bits and pieces off the bottom, and immediately scrape the bacon and sauce over the cabbage. Add the dates, toss, and season to taste with salt and pepper. Add a little more oil if the salad is too dry. Enjoy!

To take the salad to work, pack the dressed, mixed, and seasoned Krautsalat in a container. Keep it at room temperature for up to 2 hours or in the fridge for up to 24 hours.

Raw Cauliflower Carpaccio with Tangerines

SERVES 1 TO 2

FOR THE SALAD

½ small head cauliflower, cored and very thinly sliced lengthwise

2 tangerines or mandarin oranges, peeled (skin and white pith removed) and cut into slices

½ to 1 teaspoon freshly grated lemon zest

Flaky sea salt

Coarsely ground pepper

FOR THE DRESSING

1½ tablespoons olive oil, plus more as needed

2 teaspoons freshly squeezed lemon juice

Fine sea salt

Raw cauliflower tastes surprisingly subtle, considering that cooked cauliflower can be a powerful punch to the palate. Thinly cutting it like carpaccio means you need to pay attention to its delicate side. My original idea of throwing in capers, parsley, and ginger was quickly taken off the table—they would have totally overpowered it. But freshly grated lemon zest and sweet tangerines take cauliflower gently by the hand, lending a little guidance without overwhelming its mildly nutty taste. You can also use orange or blood orange, and even pomelo or grapefruit.

For the salad, layer the cauliflower and tangerines on 1 to 2 plates.

For the dressing, whisk together the olive oil and lemon juice in a small bowl and season with a little fine sea salt. Drizzle the dressing over the salad, adding a little more olive oil if it's too dry. Sprinkle with a generous amount of freshly grated lemon zest, a little flaky sea salt, and pepper; enjoy.

If you want to take the salad to work, pack the sliced cauliflower, followed by the tangerines and lemon zest, in a container. Keep the dressing separate in a jar and, if you like, keep a little flaky sea salt and coarsely ground pepper wrapped in plastic wrap for additional seasoning. Assemble right before your lunch break.

Quick Salad with Cilantro, Pink Grapefruit, and Celery

SERVES 1

FOR THE SALAD

1 large handful fresh cilantro stalks and leaves

1 celery stalk with leaves, thinly sliced

1 pink grapefruit, peeled (skin and white pith removed) and cut into segments

1 small handful cashews, roughly chopped

Piment d'Espelette (or other chili flakes)

Flaky sea salt

FOR THE DRESSING

1 tablespoon olive oil

2 teaspoons freshly squeezed lemon juice

Fine sea salt

Finely ground pepper

My friend Laurel Kratochvila, from Berlin's Fine Bagels bakery, told me about a simple snack she used to eat in Nepal of grapefruit, salt, and chili flakes. Add fresh cilantro and celery, both confident enough to handle citrus and spice, and you have a vibrant salad in less than ten minutes. Laurel points out that the saltiness is essential, as it wraps it all up. Flaky sea salt is perfect, delivering the right punch and crunch. Chopped cashews up the texture game, while piment d'Espelette, popular in France and also known as Espelette pepper, takes care of the heat. However, if France is too far or you find other chili flakes among your spice jars, go for it.

For the salad, arrange the cilantro, celery, and grapefruit on a plate and sprinkle with the cashews.

For the dressing, whisk together the olive oil and lemon juice in a small bowl and season to taste with fine sea salt and pepper. Drizzle the dressing over the salad and season to taste with chili flakes and flaky sea salt. Enjoy.

If taking the salad to work, pack the cilantro, celery, and grapefruit in a container and sprinkle with chili flakes and flaky sea salt. Keep the cashews and the dressing separate and assemble right before eating.

VEGETABLES

Gnocchi with Asparagus, Ramps, and Mustard

SERVES 2

8 ounces (225 g) trimmed green asparagus

2 tablespoons unsalted butter

9 ounces (250 g) packaged refrigerated fresh potato gnocchi

Olive oil, for cooking

1 teaspoon Dijon mustard

1 small bunch ramp or ramson leaves (or a handful of chopped chives or scallions, green parts only)

Fine sea salt

Finely ground pepper

1 to 2 tablespoons finely grated Parmesan (optional)

Daniel Schreiber is a Berlin-based author who is as inspiring for the mind as he is for the palate. When he wrote about his one-pan gnocchi with ramps, and how he doesn't chop the dainty leaves but rather uses them whole like a vegetable, I was smitten. I picked up on the idea, adding only asparagus and Dijon mustard. Daniel uses gnocchi from the store, and I do the same, which means we can indulge in this gorgeous green feast in just ten minutes. If you're looking for a more wintery treat, try the Gnocchi with Sauerkraut and Juniper Butter (page 76).

Bring a large pot of salted water to a boil and blanch the asparagus for about 3 minutes or until al dente. Drain the asparagus and briefly rinse with cold water, then cut into bite-size pieces and set aside.

In a medium, heavy pan, heat 1 tablespoon of the butter over medium-high heat until sizzling. Add the gnocchi and cook, not moving them in the first minute, then turning them occasionally, for 3 minutes or until golden brown.

Push the gnocchi to the sides of the pan and reduce the heat to medium. Add a small splash of olive oil, ½ tablespoon of the butter, and the mustard to the middle of the pan, stir, and as soon as the butter has melted, add the ramp leaves. Cook, occasionally turning and stirring the leaves in the butter, for 2 minutes or until soft.

Push the ramp leaves to the sides of the pan with the gnocchi. Add the remaining ½ tablespoon of butter and the asparagus to the middle of the pan and toss to coat, then gently mix and fold the ramp leaves, asparagus, and gnocchi. Season to taste with salt and pepper.

Divide the gnocchi and vegetables between two plates, sprinkle with a little Parmesan, and enjoy immediately.

Rösti with Pistachio-Feta Dip

SERVES 2

FOR THE DIP*

4 ounces (110 g) feta

3 to 4 tablespoons olive oil

⅓ cup (40 g) salted pistachios, plus 10 chopped pistachios for the topping

⅛ teaspoon ground cumin, plus more to taste

FOR THE RÖSTI

6 tablespoons (90 ml) olive oil

15 ounces (420 g) peeled waxy potatoes, cut into thin matchsticks

Flaky sea salt

Coarsely ground pepper

A rösti is a hearty, one-pan Swiss classic that only takes ten minutes to cook. You must be a little patient when it comes to cutting the raw potatoes—ideally, they look like matchsticks—but it's an opportunity to practice your knife skills. Once the potatoes nestle and roast in the pan, you only need to whip up a quick pistachio-feta dip, spoon it onto your crispy golden rösti, and you're done.

For the dip, purée the feta, 3 tablespoons of olive oil, ⅓ cup (40 g) of pistachios, and the cumin in a food processor or blender until smooth. Add more olive oil if the dip is too thick—it should be soft and fluffy—and season to taste with additional cumin.

For the rösti, heat 5 tablespoons (75 ml) of the olive oil in a 10-inch (25 cm) cast-iron pan over high heat. Add the potatoes, spreading them evenly and gently pushing them down with a spatula. Turn the heat down to medium-high and cook for 5 minutes, reducing the heat if the potatoes brown too quickly. Using a spatula, loosen the rösti from the sides of the pan and lift gently off the bottom. Cover the pan with a large lid, then carefully and quickly flip the pan over. Keep the rösti on the lid while you add the remaining 1 tablespoon of olive oil to the pan, then slide the rösti off the lid into the pan. Cook for about 5 minutes or until the potatoes are golden brown and crispy on the bottom. Loosen the rösti from the sides and bottom of the pan and slide onto a large plate. Season to taste with salt and pepper. Top with a generous dollop of the pistachio-feta dip, sprinkle with the chopped pistachios, and serve.

* You can use leftover feta dip as a spread on bread.

Roasted Mediterranean Vegetables with Feta and Fresh Herbs

SERVES 2 TO 3

1 small eggplant, cut into quarters lengthwise and thinly sliced

1 medium zucchini, cut in half lengthwise and thinly sliced

½ medium red bell pepper, cut into cubes

½ medium yellow bell pepper, cut into cubes

¼ cup (60 ml) olive oil

Flaky sea salt

Coarsely ground pepper

1 (7-ounce / 200 g) thick slice feta

6 large Kalamata olives

1 small bunch fresh thyme

5 small sprigs fresh rosemary

⅓ to ½ baguette, for serving

The basic formula for this dish is genius—and has become quite popular in the last couple of years—and I will be forever thankful that my aunt Ursula first brought it into my life. Place a thick slice of feta in a baking dish, pile lots of vegetables on top, and roast it in the oven for about half an hour. It works with winter squash like butternut (page 95), a favorite in the cooler months, and it's unbeatable in summer with zucchini, bell pepper, and eggplant. Sprinkled with fresh herbs and served with a crunchy baguette—and maybe a glass of crisp white wine—it's lunch perfection for the hedonistic weekday soul. You can also prepare it in advance and enjoy it cold the next day, piled on a slice of bread.

Preheat the oven to 400°F (200°C).

In a medium baking dish, toss the eggplant, zucchini, and red and yellow bell peppers with the olive oil and season with salt and pepper.

Place the feta underneath the vegetables in the middle of the baking dish, then sprinkle the vegetables with the olives, thyme, and rosemary. Roast for 35 to 45 minutes or until the zucchini and eggplant are tender. Enjoy warm, with a fresh baguette, or cold the next day, stuffed into a baguette sandwich.

Chopped Cauliflower with Smoked Fish, Lemon, and Capers

SERVES 2

1 pound (450 g) cored cauliflower, broken into large chunks

3 tablespoons olive oil, plus 2 teaspoons for finishing

2 teaspoons freshly grated lemon zest, plus more for serving

1 tablespoon freshly squeezed lemon juice

Nutmeg, preferably freshly grated

Fine sea salt

Finely ground pepper

5 ounces (140 g) smoked fish fillets, such as trout, eel, or halibut, cut into chunks

2 to 3 teaspoons capers, rinsed

Chopped, blanched cauliflower may not sound exciting, but add lemon, capers, and smoked fish—such as trout, eel, or halibut—and it's a whole other story. It's not really a surprise that the pale head manages to stand its ground next to such strong counterparts. Cooked cauliflower can be assertive and rock star–like if you let it. This dish is loud and a little extravagant, even if you keep it vegetarian and leave out the fish, which won't harm the experience in the least.

Bring a medium pot of salted water to a boil, add the cauliflower, and cook for about 12 minutes or until soft. Drain the cauliflower and briefly rinse with cold water, then return it to the pot. Add 3 tablespoons of olive oil, 2 teaspoons of lemon zest, and the lemon juice. Using a plain butter knife, chop the cauliflower until it's quite smooth and resembles a fine chunky mash. Season to taste with nutmeg, salt, and pepper; mind that the capers and smoked fish will also add saltiness.

Divide the cauliflower between two bowls and arrange the fish on top, then drizzle each portion with 1 teaspoon of olive oil and sprinkle with the capers, a little pepper, and ½ to 1 teaspoon of lemon zest. Enjoy warm or cold.

One-Pan Butter Beans and Spinach with Ricotta and Lemon

SERVES 2

4 slices ciabatta

Olive oil, for cooking

1¼ cups (250 g) drained and rinsed canned butter beans (lima beans)

Fine sea salt

Finely ground pepper

3 ounces (85 g) baby spinach (or trimmed, chopped regular spinach)

3 tablespoons freshly squeezed lemon juice

2 to 3 tablespoons fresh ricotta

1 to 2 teaspoons freshly grated lemon zest

A hot pan and a can of butter beans are a lunch match made in heaven. This approach works incredibly well for the One-Pan Butter Beans and Tomatoes with Arugula and Sourdough Bread (page 98), and it's just as glorious in this recipe. You can sit in front of a bowl filled with crisped golden beans, wilted baby spinach, and lemony ricotta in less than ten minutes—how convenient is that? Piled onto a slice of pan-toasted ciabatta, it becomes a luscious little bite. The beans and spinach are smooth, the ricotta makes it creamy but not heavy, and the lemon's juice and zest shine above everything. It's bold, fresh, and sour—and so quick to prepare.

Heat a medium, heavy pan over high heat without adding any fat. When the pan is very hot, add the ciabatta and toast, flipping once, for 1 to 2 minutes or until golden brown and crunchy. Transfer the ciabatta to a plate, then carefully wipe out the pan with a paper towel and immediately place it over medium-high heat.

Add a splash of olive oil and the butter beans to the pan, then season with a little salt and pepper, stir, and cook for 1 to 2 minutes or until golden and a little crispy. Add the spinach and lemon juice, then drizzle with a little olive oil, stir gently, and season to taste with salt and pepper. Cook for about 30 seconds or until the spinach starts to wilt (regular spinach will need a little longer). Plop dollops of ricotta on top and sprinkle with the lemon zest. Serve warm—or cold—with the toasted ciabatta.

Roasted Kale, Squash, and Shallots with Pear and Stilton

SERVES 2

FOR THE VEGETABLES

12 ounces (340 g) seeded squash, preferably peeled butternut or Hokkaido with skin, cut into 1-inch (2.5 cm) wedges

4 shallots, unpeeled

4 tablespoons (60 ml) olive oil

Flaky sea salt

Finely ground pepper

6 ounces (170 g) trimmed kale leaves

1 large, tender pear, cored and cut into thin wedges

2 ounces (60 g) Stilton or Roquefort, crumbled

FOR THE DRESSING

3 tablespoons olive oil

2 tablespoons white balsamic vinegar

1 teaspoon Dijon mustard

Fine sea salt

Finely ground pepper

Imagine a cold winter day, the air crisp and clear but the light dim and gloomy. Wouldn't it be nice to have a plate in front of you packed with roasted vegetables that bring bright colors and flavors into your life? It's so easy: Roast kale, squash, and shallots on one baking sheet for less than thirty minutes, and then layer the flavorsome bunch with tender pear and Stilton and drizzle with a golden mustard vinaigrette. It's hearty and cozy, yet thanks to the vibrant vegetables, there's something light and fresh about this recipe. You can see it as a warm or cold salad, as a side dish for Bratwurst, or as a very nourishing and satisfying vegetarian lunch.

Preheat the oven to 400°F (200°C).

For the vegetables, spread the squash and shallots on a large baking sheet, drizzle with 2 tablespoons of the olive oil, and toss to coat, then season with a little flaky sea salt and pepper and roast for 15 minutes. While the squash and shallots are roasting, toss the kale with the remaining 2 tablespoons of olive oil in a large bowl and season with salt and pepper. After 15 minutes, gently flip the squash and shallots, then push them to one half of the baking sheet and add the kale to the other half, spreading it out evenly. Continue roasting for 10 to 15 minutes or until the kale starts to soften. Remove from the oven and set aside. Let the shallots cool for a few minutes, then peel and cut in half lengthwise.

For the dressing, whisk together the olive oil, vinegar, and mustard in a small bowl and season to taste with fine sea salt and pepper.

Divide the kale, squash, pear, and shallots between 2 large plates. Sprinkle with the Stilton, drizzle with the dressing, and enjoy warm or cold.

Mashed Celeriac with Seared Apple and Thyme Butter

SERVES 2

1 pound (450 g) peeled celeriac, cut into cubes

1 bay leaf

¼ cup (60 ml) whole milk

2 generous tablespoons unsalted butter

Nutmeg, preferably freshly grated

Fine sea salt

Finely ground pepper

Olive oil, for searing

1 large tart, firm apple, cored and cut into 8 wedges

1 tablespoon fresh thyme leaves

Himmel und Erde, meaning "heaven and earth"—technically *Erde* means "soil"—also refers to a popular dish in many parts of my home country. It features the frugal produce that has always played an important role in traditional German cooking: potatoes and apples. One grows in the ground and the other above it. We can pick up on this idea but mix it up by swapping the potato for celeriac. Celeriac—also called celery root—makes a wonderful peppery, chunky purée, which is a perfect bed for the good old apple. Seared briefly in a hot pan, the fruit is still firm yet the flavor a bit more concentrated. You can keep this dish vegetarian or enjoy it with a well-seasoned coarse sausage. Having it with Blutwurst (blood sausage) on the side follows hearty German tradition, as does briefly seared liver, which has been my favorite since childhood.

Bring a medium pot of salted water to a boil, add the celeriac and bay leaf, and cook for about 12 minutes or until very soft. Remove and discard the bay leaf, then drain the celeriac, briefly rinse with cold water, and return to the pot. Add the milk, 1 tablespoon of the butter, and a little nutmeg, salt, and pepper. Using a masher, mash and beat the celeriac until smooth but still a bit chunky. Season to taste with additional nutmeg, salt, and pepper, cover, and set aside.

In a small, heavy pan, heat a little olive oil over high heat. Add the apple wedges and sear, turning them once, for about 2 minutes or until golden brown and still firm; mind that they don't burn. Transfer the apple wedges to a plate, but keep the pan on high heat. Add the remaining 1 generous tablespoon of butter and a pinch of salt to the pan. As soon as it's sizzling, stir in the thyme and cook for just a few seconds; remove the pan from the heat.

Divide the mashed celeriac between two bowls, arrange the apple wedges on top, and drizzle with the thyme butter. Serve immediately.

Gnocchi with Sauerkraut and Juniper Butter

SERVES 2

2½ tablespoons unsalted butter

7 large juniper berries, crushed with a mortar and pestle, or 1 very finely crushed bay leaf

9 ounces (250 g) packaged refrigerated fresh potato gnocchi

5 ounces (140 g) drained and squeezed jarred or canned sauerkraut

Fine sea salt

Finely ground pepper

In Germany, we usually eat sauerkraut with mashed potatoes, but why shouldn't potato gnocchi be just as good? As much as I enjoy making gnocchi from scratch for a relaxed weekend lunch or dinner, I can also totally indulge in potato dumplings from the store without remorse. And store-bought refrigerated fresh gnocchi don't even need to be boiled; you can cook them in a pan, with a little butter, and turn them into crispy golden pillows within minutes. Infuse the butter with crushed juniper berries—or bay leaf if you can't get your hands on juniper—and mix in drained uncooked sauerkraut, and you'll take a German classic to the next level. The fermented kraut is used sparingly here, simply dappling the gnocchi and functioning a bit like a seasoning. We are going for little bites to add flavor without smothering the gnocchi. Although one person could wolf the whole recipe down, I recommend sharing it.

In a medium, heavy pan, heat 1 tablespoon of the butter and the juniper berries over medium-high heat until foaming and sizzling. Add the gnocchi and cook, not moving them in the first minute, then turning them occasionally, for 3 minutes or until golden brown. Transfer the gnocchi to a plate.

Return the pan to medium-high heat, add 1 tablespoon of the butter and the sauerkraut, and cook, stirring, for 2 minutes. Push the sauerkraut to the sides of the pan and add the remaining ½ tablespoon of butter to the middle of the pan. When the butter has melted, return the gnocchi to the pan and gently mix with the sauerkraut. Season to taste with salt and pepper and immediately divide between two plates. You can eat leftovers the next day, reheating them in a pan over medium-high heat, without adding any fat, and stirring constantly.

Fried Potato Wedges with Fava Beans and Fennel

SERVES 2

5 ounces (140 g) fresh or frozen shelled fava beans

Olive oil, for sautéing

1 tablespoon fennel seeds, lightly crushed with a mortar and pestle

½ medium fennel bulb, cored and thinly sliced lengthwise

Flaky sea salt

Coarsely ground pepper

14 ounces (400 g) small waxy potatoes, boiled, cut into quarters, and chilled

During a chat over a perfect cappuccino, my friend Gabi pointed out that the combination of fava beans and fennel is a rather fine one. You can toss the cooked vegetables with only olive oil and flaky sea salt or use them to lighten up a pan of crispy fried potato wedges. I blanch the beans and briefly sauté the fennel to keep it al dente. Adding fennel seeds enhances the sweet aroma of anise, which charms the beans and the hearty potatoes. Fresh green fava beans—or broad beans—appear at farmers' markets in spring. However, you can also use canned or frozen fava beans. I keep a large bag of them in my freezer all year round.

Bring a small pot of salted water to a boil and blanch the beans for about 5 minutes or until tender. Drain the beans, briefly rinse with cold water, and transfer to a medium bowl.

In a large, heavy pan, heat a generous splash of olive oil over medium-high heat. Add the fennel seeds and cook, stirring, for 20 seconds. Add the fennel bulb and sauté, stirring occasionally, for about 4 minutes or until golden and al dente. Season to taste with salt and pepper, then transfer to the bowl with the beans and mix gently.

Place the pan over medium-high to high heat and add a generous splash of olive oil. Add half the potatoes and fry them, turning twice and reducing the heat if they brown too quickly, for about 3 minutes or until golden brown and very crispy on all sides. Season to taste with salt and pepper, then transfer to a plate. Add a splash of olive oil to the pan if it's too dry, then fry the remaining potatoes in the same way. When they are done, return all the potatoes, along with the fennel and beans, to the pan, layering the vegetables gently, and adjust the seasoning. Serve immediately.

Beluga Lentils with Parsnip, Plums, and Tahini

SERVES 2

⅔ cup (140 g) lentils, preferably beluga (no soaking required)

6 sprigs fresh thyme

2 small bay leaves

2 teaspoons balsamic vinegar

Olive oil, for dressing and searing

Fine sea salt

Finely ground pepper

4 ounces (110 g) peeled parsnip, cut in half lengthwise and cut into ¼-inch (0.5 cm) slices

2 large dark plums, pitted and cut into quarters

1 teaspoon honey

2 tablespoons tahini

2 tablespoons water

Beluga lentils look like little black pearls. They hold their shape when you cook them and taste wonderfully nutty. Although rather rustic and frugal, they encourage the cook to come up with some drama in the kitchen—if only visually. Blanched peppery parsnip and seared plums rise to the occasion. They both deliver the right amount of depth and contrast to keep this dish exciting but not pretentious. A thick tahini drizzle, also on the nutty side, pulls it all together without distracting. You can replace the plums with any fruit that lends acidity, such as nectarine or apple wedges, or even grapes or berries.

Place the lentils in a medium saucepan with plenty of (unsalted) water, add the thyme and bay leaves, and bring to a boil. Reduce the heat and simmer, adding more water, if necessary, for about 20 minutes or until al dente (or follow the package instructions). The lentils shouldn't be dry; there should be a little cooking liquid left. Remove and discard the herbs, then stir in 1 teaspoon of the vinegar and a little olive oil, and season to taste with salt and pepper.

Meanwhile, bring a small pot of salted water to a boil and blanch the parsnip for 4 to 5 minutes or until just tender. Drain the parsnip and briefly rinse with cold water, then transfer to a plate.

In a medium, heavy pan, heat a few drops of olive oil over medium-high heat. Add the plums, cut-side down, and sear, turning once, for 2 minutes or until golden brown; they should still hold their shape. Add the remaining 1 teaspoon of vinegar, the honey, and a pinch of salt and cook, gently stirring, for 1 minute.

In a small bowl, whisk together the tahini, water, and a pinch of salt. Divide the lentils between two bowls and arrange the parsnip and plums on top. Drizzle with the tahini sauce and sprinkle with a little pepper. Enjoy warm.

Roasted Broccoli and Apples
with Mustard–Lemon Dressing

SERVES 2

12 ounces (340 g) trimmed broccoli florets, cut in half lengthwise

4 tablespoons (60 ml) olive oil

2 small, sour apples, cored and cut into quarters

1 medium lemon, cut into 6 wedges

Flaky sea salt

Coarsely ground pepper

1 tablespoon freshly squeezed lemon juice

1 teaspoon Dijon mustard

Broccoli isn't the first vegetable I grab at my supermarket. I don't dislike it, but it doesn't easily inspire my creativity. However, it's not impossible; my mind just has to work a little harder. Roasting the green florets in the oven—my favorite technique for all kinds of brassicas—gives it a smoky touch but also calls for additional fresh flavors. Fruity and sour, that's what we're looking for here. Broccoli florets, apples, and lemon wedges are roasted together and then drizzled with a simple Dijon mustard–lemon dressing. It's an easy sheet-pan meal. You can eat it warm, straight from the pan, with a bowl of buttered rice on the side, or enjoy it as a cold salad.

Preheat the oven to 450°F (230°C).

Spread the broccoli florets on a baking sheet, drizzle with 2 tablespoons of the olive oil, and toss to combine. In a medium bowl, toss the apples with 1 tablespoon of the olive oil, then arrange the apples and lemon wedges between the broccoli florets. Season with a little salt and pepper and roast, without flipping, for 15 to 20 minutes or until the broccoli is golden brown and tender.

Whisk together the remaining 1 tablespoon of olive oil, lemon juice, and mustard in a small bowl and drizzle over the roasted broccoli and apples. Divide between two plates and squeeze some juice from the roasted lemon wedges over the vegetables and fruit. Enjoy warm or as a cold salad.

Mediterranean Mashed Potatoes
with Blanched Spinach

SERVES 2

1 pound (450 g) peeled
waxy potatoes

4 ounces (110 g) baby
spinach (or trimmed
regular spinach)

4 tablespoons (60 ml)
olive oil

Nutmeg, preferably
freshly grated

Flaky sea salt

Finely ground pepper

OPTIONAL SEASONINGS
(choose only one)

1½ teaspoons freshly
grated lemon zest

1½ teaspoons fennel seeds,
crushed with a mortar
and pestle

1½ teaspoons coriander
seeds, crushed with a
mortar and pestle

There's something utterly satisfying about the familiar simplicity of good produce, olive oil, and sea salt. Boiled potatoes,
chopped and broken with a knife rather than crushed with a
masher, and mixed with olive oil instead of milk and butter, is
one of my favorite dishes. I call them Mediterranean mashed
potatoes, and usually season them with just flaky sea salt or,
when I'm in a bolder mood, crushed fennel seeds or coriander
seeds. Stirring in freshly grated lemon zest turns this mash into
the perfect side for seafood.

In a medium pot, cover the potatoes with salted water
and bring to a boil. Reduce the heat, cover, and simmer
for 18 to 20 minutes or until tender. Drain the potatoes
and return them to the pot.

Meanwhile, bring a medium pot of salted water to a boil
and blanch the baby spinach for 30 seconds or until
tender (if you use regular spinach, blanch it for about
1½ minutes). Transfer the spinach to a colander, drain,
and quickly rinse with cold water. Leave the spinach
in the colander to cool for 1 minute, then squeeze it a
bit and return it to the pot; roughly chop the blanched
regular spinach. Stir in 1 tablespoon of the olive oil and
season to taste with nutmeg, salt, and pepper.

When the potatoes are done, add the remaining
3 tablespoons of olive oil and a little salt to the pot. If
you want to use additional seasoning, add the lemon
zest, fennel seeds, or coriander seeds now. Using
a plain butter knife, break the potatoes into small
chunks—they should be smooth but still a bit chunky.
Season to taste with salt.

Arrange the mashed potatoes and spinach next to each
other on plates and enjoy warm—or even cold.

Caponata with Fennel Seeds

SERVES 4 TO 6

Olive oil, for sautéing

3 small whole shallots

2 large cloves garlic, cut in half

2 tablespoons fennel seeds (whole, not crushed)

1 small eggplant, cut into quarters lengthwise and thinly sliced

1 medium zucchini, cut in half lengthwise and thinly sliced

1 medium red bell pepper, cut into cubes

1 medium yellow bell pepper, cut into cubes

1¾ pounds (800 g) canned whole peeled tomatoes, chopped

2 tablespoons tomato paste

1 tablespoon balsamic vinegar, plus more to taste

3 small bay leaves

Fine sea salt

Finely ground pepper

1 small bunch fresh flat-leaf parsley

1 loaf ciabatta, cut into thick slices, for serving

In the Mediterranean, you would never cook a small amount of caponata. That's a rule. You can keep these stewed vegetables in the fridge for days—you don't even need to warm them up, as they taste just as good cold. You share your caponata with friends and family or scoop it up with a slice of bread when you feel a sudden craving at noon—or midnight. With a loaf of ciabatta and a glass of red wine on the table, it's one of the best summer meals I can think of. If you have ripe fresh tomatoes on hand, use them, but to satisfy my appetite for caponata all year round, I started using canned tomatoes—always whole peeled tomatoes, never crushed. Their taste is more concentrated. In this recipe, I enhance the caponata with a good amount of fennel seeds. If you're not in the mood for their licoricey quality, leave them out, but don't even bother using just a pinch—it would vanish.

In a large, heavy pot, heat a generous splash of olive oil over medium-high heat. Add the shallots and garlic and sauté, stirring, for about 3 minutes or until golden. Add the fennel seeds and cook, stirring constantly, for 10 seconds. Add another splash of olive oil, along with the eggplant, zucchini, and red and yellow bell peppers, and mix well with the fennel seeds. Cook, stirring, for 3 minutes. Add the tomatoes, tomato paste, vinegar, and bay leaves, mix well, and season with salt and pepper. Add the bunch of parsley, gently pushing it into the vegetables, and bring to a boil. Reduce the heat, cover, and simmer, stirring occasionally, for 30 to 40 minutes or until the eggplant and zucchini are soft. Remove and discard the parsley, shallots, garlic, and bay leaves and season to taste with salt, pepper, and additional vinegar.

Serve the caponata, warm or cold, with thick slices of ciabatta. You can keep the caponata, covered, in the fridge for up to 3 days.

Polenta with Coriander Bell Peppers

SERVES 2

FOR THE POLENTA

1 cup (240 ml) whole milk

1 cup (240 ml) water, plus more as needed

2 tablespoons olive oil

1 teaspoon fine sea salt

¾ cup (120 g) fine polenta

FOR THE BELL PEPPERS

Olive oil, for cooking

1 tablespoon coriander seeds, lightly crushed with a mortar and pestle

1 medium yellow bell pepper, cut into very thin slices

1 medium red bell pepper, cut into very thin slices

Fine sea salt

Finely ground pepper

1 teaspoon balsamic vinegar

This dish combines two lunch gems: smooth polenta and sautéed bell peppers. Polenta cooked with milk, water, and a little olive oil is the most satisfying bed for all sorts of vegetables. It's neither too dominant nor too submissive. No matter what you add—even a rich ragù—golden polenta will have a presence. Red and yellow bell peppers, cooked with coriander seeds, are as tasty as a ragù but not as heavy. They are juicy, sweet, and soak up the citrusy aroma of the crunchy seeds. This is a comforting dish—and quick to prepare—yet it still manages to bring a little excitement to your lunch break.

For the polenta, bring the milk, water, olive oil, and salt to a boil in a medium saucepan. Reduce the heat to medium-low, add the polenta, and whisk until combined. Cook the polenta, stirring occasionally and adding a little more water whenever it starts to thicken, for 10 minutes; the polenta should be thick, smooth, and creamy. Cover and set aside.

Meanwhile, for the bell peppers, in a medium, heavy pan, heat a splash of olive oil over medium-high heat. Add the coriander seeds and cook, stirring, for 10 seconds. Add the yellow and red bell peppers, mix with the coriander seeds, and season with a little salt and pepper. Sauté the peppers, stirring occasionally and reducing the heat to medium, if necessary, for about 12 minutes or until the peppers are tender. Stir in the vinegar and 1 tablespoon of olive oil, season to taste with salt and pepper, and take the pan off the heat.

Divide the polenta, bell peppers, and coriander seeds between two plates and enjoy immediately.

Roasted Brussels Sprouts with Orange and Cinnamon

SERVES 2 TO 3

1¼ pounds (550 g) trimmed Brussels sprouts, cut in half

¼ cup (60 ml) olive oil

3 tablespoons freshly squeezed orange juice

2 teaspoons ground cinnamon

1 teaspoon granulated sugar

Flaky sea salt

1 large orange, cut into 8 wedges

Brussels sprouts are not a side dish here—they take center stage. These little cabbages really need a potent punch from other ingredients and confident seasoning. The sweet acidity of the orange and the right amount of salt cut through their cabagge-y tone. Adding a generous hit of ground cinnamon leads to a pungent yet surprisingly harmonious result. I like it to be very present, but if you're sensitive to the warming spice, halve the amount and add more once the Brussels sprouts are roasted. Be sure to squeeze the roasted oranges and use their juice boldly. You can serve this recipe as a warm or cold salad or combine it with the Mediterranean Mashed Potatoes (page 85) or Lentil Salad (page 53). You should also try it as a topping for the Tahini Oats (page 255). It may sound a bit too adventurous, but they are practically made for each other.

Preheat the oven to 425°F (220°C).

Spread the Brussels sprouts in a medium baking dish. Whisk together the olive oil, orange juice, and cinnamon, then pour over the Brussels sprouts and toss to combine. Sprinkle with the sugar, season generously with salt, and arrange the orange wedges on top. Roast for 10 minutes, gently stir, and continue roasting, stirring every 5 minutes or so, for 15 to 20 minutes or until golden brown and al dente.

For serving, generously squeeze the juice from the roasted orange wedges over the Brussels sprouts and season to taste with salt. Enjoy warm or cold.

Roasted Eggplant with Greek Skordalia

SERVES 2

FOR THE EGGPLANT

1 medium eggplant (about
9 ounces / 250 g), cut into
½-inch-thick (1.25 cm) circles

¼ cup (60 ml) olive oil

Flaky sea salt

Coarsely ground pepper

FOR THE SKORDALIA

8 ounces (225 g) peeled
starchy potatoes

6 large cloves garlic,
unpeeled

¼ cup (60 ml) olive oil

1 teaspoon freshly grated
lemon zest, plus more
for serving

2 teaspoons freshly
squeezed lemon juice

Fine sea salt

Coarsely ground pepper

The next time you have some boiled potatoes lying around and don't know what to do with them, purée them with a good amount of blanched garlic and olive oil and you will have skordalia. Although this famous Greek dip can be mistaken for mashed potatoes, you really should treat it as a dip. Olive oil is used generously and eating a whole plateful of skordalia might be a bit overwhelming, but a forkful lifts up every roasted vegetable. I like to boost this silky spread with lemon zest and juice, giving it a lighter feeling.

Preheat the oven to 425°F (220°C).

For the eggplant, in a medium baking dish, toss the eggplant and olive oil. Arrange the eggplant circles side by side and season with flaky sea salt and pepper. Roast for about 20 minutes or until golden; mind that they don't burn. Flip the eggplant and continue roasting for 10 minutes or until golden brown and soft.

Meanwhile, for the skordalia, cover the potatoes with salted water in a small pot and bring to a boil. Reduce the heat, cover, and simmer for 18 to 20 minutes or until tender. Drain the potatoes, transfer to a plate, and let them cool for a few minutes; you can use them cold or warm.

In a small saucepan, bring a little salted water to a boil and blanch the garlic for 5 minutes. Drain the garlic and briefly rinse with cold water, then peel and transfer to a blender or food processor. Add the potatoes, olive oil, lemon zest, and lemon juice, briefly purée for about 20 seconds or until smooth but not gooey, and season to taste with fine sea salt and pepper.

Divide the eggplant slices between two plates and place a dollop of skordalia next to them. Sprinkle with a little pepper and lemon zest and enjoy warm or cold.

Roasted Squash with Feta and Sage

SERVES 2 TO 3

1⅓ pounds (600 g) seeded squash, preferably peeled butternut or Hokkaido with skin, cut into 1-inch (2.5 cm) wedges

5 tablespoons (75 ml) olive oil

1 (7-ounce / 200 g) thick slice feta

Flaky sea salt

Coarsely ground pepper

30 large fresh sage leaves

If the Roasted Mediterranean Vegetables with Feta and Fresh Herbs (page 66) embrace summer and its produce, here we celebrate the colder seasons. Roasted winter squash and sage assure a comforting lunch, while the slice of feta lying underneath is proof this cheese goes well with any vegetable. It's tangy, salty, and adds depth to the sweet and silky squash. This dish is great with just ciabatta on the side, but if you are in the mood for meat, throw some lamb chops in the pan (page 235). You can use leftovers for a salad the next day, layered with colorful lettuce leaves (page 28), or cut the squash and feta into chunky cubes and fold them into pasta. Puréeing the roasted vegetable and squeezing it into a sandwich (page 152) is also delicious. Always fry fresh sage leaves, as they lose their crispness when they've sat around for too long.

Preheat the oven to 400°F (200°C).

In a medium baking dish, toss the squash with 3 tablespoons of the olive oil. Place the feta underneath the squash in the middle of the baking dish. Season with salt and pepper and roast for about 30 minutes or until the squash is golden and tender.

While the squash is roasting, heat the remaining 2 tablespoons of olive oil in a medium pot over medium-high heat. Add half of the sage leaves, spreading them out evenly, and cook, stirring gently, for about 30 seconds or until golden, green, and crispy. Transfer to a plate, arranging the leaves next to each other, then cook the remaining sage leaves in the same way.

Sprinkle the roasted squash and feta with the sage leaves and enjoy.

Roasted Rhubarb and Green Beans with Ricotta

SERVES 2

8 ounces (225 g) trimmed
romano beans or green beans

3½ tablespoons olive oil

8 ounces (225 g) rhubarb,
cut in half lengthwise

Flaky sea salt

Finely ground pepper

1 small bunch fresh thyme

1½ teaspoons white
balsamic vinegar

½ teaspoon Dijon mustard

Fine sea salt

¼ cup (60 g) fresh ricotta

If you're not up for a trip off the beaten track, skip this recipe. It's adventurous and treats rhubarb as a vegetable, taking full advantage of its tart quality. Romano or green beans and ricotta join in to create a dish with unusual beauty. Try it on an early spring day when you're in the mood for something new. I like it warm or cold, with crunchy crostini on the side, or on top of creamy polenta (page 89). It surprises the taste buds, reminding us how much fun it is to discover uncharted flavor experiences.

Preheat the oven to 400°F (200°C).

Bring a large pot of salted water to a boil and blanch the beans for 4 minutes or until just tender. Drain the beans and briefly rinse with cold water. Transfer the beans to a medium baking dish, toss with 1 tablespoon of the olive oil, and spread out evenly.

Cut the rhubarb crosswise into long pieces that fit in your baking dish. On a large plate, toss the rhubarb with 1 tablespoon of the olive oil, then arrange it on top of the beans. Season with flaky sea salt and pepper, sprinkle with the thyme sprigs, and roast for 20 minutes or until the rhubarb is soft.

Whisk together the remaining 1½ tablespoons of olive oil with the vinegar and mustard in a small bowl and season to taste with fine sea salt and pepper. Plop the ricotta on top of the rhubarb and beans and drizzle with the dressing. Enjoy warm or cold.

One-Pan Butter Beans and Tomatoes with Arugula and Sourdough Bread

SERVES 2

1 thick slice white sourdough bread with crust (around 4 ounces / 110 g), cut into chunky cubes

2 tablespoons olive oil, plus more for drizzling

12 grape or cherry tomatoes

1¼ cups (250 g) drained and rinsed canned butter beans (lima beans)

1 teaspoon balsamic vinegar

Fine sea salt

Finely ground pepper

1 large handful fresh arugula leaves

1 to 2 tablespoons finely grated Parmesan

A scorching hot, heavy skillet can create kitchen wonders. It's like a barbecue grill, just indoors and without charcoal. Small tomatoes, such as cherry or grape, and sourdough bread cubes briefly visit the dry pan—no fat required—giving them a few blisters and a subtle smoky flavor. Canned butter beans also join in and crisp in a splash of olive oil, before fresh arugula leaves and Parmesan smoothly melt into this ten-minute, one-pan wonder. The One-Pan Butter Beans and Spinach with Ricotta and Lemon (page 71) uses the same technique and leads to an equally satisfying result—in case you're getting hooked.

On a large plate, drizzle the bread cubes with 1 tablespoon of the olive oil. Heat a medium, heavy pan over high heat without adding any fat. When the pan is very hot, add the bread cubes and toast, turning constantly, for about 2 minutes or until crunchy and golden brown with a few dark freckles. Transfer the bread to a plate.

Carefully wipe out the pan with a paper towel, then place the pan back over high heat. Add the tomatoes and sear, shaking the pan and reducing the heat to medium-high, if necessary, for 2 to 3 minutes or until the skins are partly freckled and blistered. Gently squeeze the tomatoes a little to burst their skins, then push the tomatoes to the sides of the pan. Add the remaining 1 tablespoon of olive oil and the beans to the middle of the pan. Sear the beans, stirring constantly, for 1 minute, then add the vinegar and season to taste with salt and pepper. Gently fold the arugula into the beans and tomatoes, then drizzle with a little olive oil, add the toasted bread, and sprinkle with the Parmesan. Enjoy warm or cold!

Sweet Potato and Parsnip Gratin
with Gorgonzola and Thyme

SERVES 2

14 ounces (400 g) peeled sweet potato, cut into ⅛-inch-thick (0.3 cm) circles

7 ounces (200 g) peeled parsnip, cut into ⅛-inch-thick (0.3 cm) circles

¼ cup (60 ml) olive oil

Flaky sea salt

Coarsely ground pepper

3 ounces (85 g) Gorgonzola, cut into small cubes

1 small bunch fresh thyme, plus 1 tablespoon fresh thyme leaves

Sweet potato and parsnip are both strong autumn flavors—one sweet and the other a little peppery with a hint of warming spice. Together they make a fabulous gratin, one that's tender, not crisp. Sliced and layered, the vegetables welcome creamy Gorgonzola to melt and spread piquant notes. Make sure the roots are cut thinly; this is the perfect recipe to get out your mandoline to save time. However, a sharp, long knife works just as well—it only takes a little longer.

Preheat the oven to 400°F (200°C).

In a 12-inch (30 cm) quiche dish, drizzle the sweet potato and parsnip with the olive oil and toss to coat. Arrange the vegetables in overlapping layers, season with salt and pepper, and sprinkle with the Gorgonzola and thyme sprigs. Roast for about 30 minutes or until the vegetables are tender. Sprinkle with the fresh thyme leaves and enjoy warm or cold.

Red Lentils with Spinach and Spiced Feta

SERVES 2 TO 3

3 tablespoons olive oil

2 teaspoons freshly squeezed lemon juice

¼ teaspoon ground cumin

¼ teaspoon ground cinnamon

¼ teaspoon ground cardamom

5 ounces (140 g) feta, broken into small chunks

1 cup (220 g) red lentils (no soaking required)

2½ cups (600 ml) unsalted homemade or quality store-bought vegetable broth

2 small bay leaves

4 ounces (110 g) baby spinach (or trimmed, chopped regular spinach)

Fine sea salt

Finely ground pepper

Lentils can handle bold flavors surprisingly well, so it's nearly impossible to overpower them. Paired with spices, herbs, or cheese—no matter what the cook comes up with—lentils stand their ground. Here, we use salty feta, marinated in olive oil and spiced up with ground cumin, cardamom, and cinnamon. Baby spinach leaves, much like the lentils, aren't bothered by this powerful spice attack. It's all beautifully balanced yet vibrant.

Whisk together the olive oil, 1 teaspoon of the lemon juice, the cumin, cinnamon, and cardamom in a medium bowl. Add the feta and gently toss to coat; set the bowl aside.

Place the lentils in a medium pot, add the broth and bay leaves, and bring to a boil. Reduce the heat and simmer, uncovered, for about 8 minutes or until tender (or follow the package instructions); the lentils shouldn't be dry, and there should be a little cooking liquid left. Remove and discard the bay leaves, then stir in the spinach and cook for 1 minute. Take the pot off the heat. Add the remaining 1 teaspoon of lemon juice and 2 teaspoons of the spiced oil from the marinated feta; season to taste with salt and pepper.

Divide the lentils and spinach among bowls and arrange the marinated feta on top. Drizzle with a little spiced oil from the feta and enjoy warm.

Bacon and Egg with Seared Belgian Endive

SERVES 1

Olive oil, for cooking

2 to 3 slices bacon

1 medium head Belgian endive, cut in half lengthwise

Fine sea salt

Finely ground pepper

1 to 2 large eggs

1 slice white sourdough bread

1 teaspoon fresh marjoram, thyme, or chopped basil leaves

Fried eggs with bacon is one of the most comforting—and quickest—meals to cook in a pan. While it's very satisfying, it often leaves me longing for some veggies. So here, we use the bacon fat in the pan to sauté a head of Belgian endive. The outer leaves soften, but the center stays al dente. Sprinkled with fresh marjoram, thyme, or basil, the dish becomes more complex yet not complicated.

In a small, heavy pan, heat a little olive oil over medium-high heat. Add the bacon and cook for a few minutes or until golden brown and crispy. Transfer the bacon to a large plate, but leave the fat in the pan and the pan over medium-high heat. Add the Belgian endive to the pan and sauté for 1½ to 2 minutes per side or until golden brown and al dente. Season to taste with salt and pepper, then transfer to the plate with the bacon.

Place the pan over medium heat, add the eggs, and fry to the desired doneness. Season to taste with salt and pepper, then transfer to the plate with the bacon and endive.

Place the pan over medium-high heat, add the bread, and toast for a few minutes per side or until golden and crunchy.

Sprinkle the Belgian endive, egg, and bacon with the marjoram and enjoy with the toasted bread.

Sweet Potato with Seared Plums and Olives

SERVES 1

Olive oil, for searing

2 large dark plums, pitted and cut into quarters

Fine sea salt

1½ teaspoons coriander seeds, finely crushed with a mortar and pestle

7 ounces (200 g) peeled sweet potato, quartered lengthwise and cut into ¼-inch (0.5 cm) slices

Finely ground pepper

¼ cup (60 ml) freshly squeezed orange juice

4 black olives, preferably Kalamata

If you don't like black olives, there's no need to skip this recipe. Just leave them out. If you keep them in, be prepared for fireworks of bold flavor. Fleshy sweet potato slices, cooked in orange juice for just five minutes, are pleasantly fruity. Together with coriander seeds, they unfold more of their sweet than their earthy side. Briefly seared dark plums join in, covering the sour range of the taste map, and black Kalamata olives add a delicious bitter note. This unusual dish screams, but that's good if you're up for it.

In a medium, heavy pan, heat a small splash of olive oil over medium-high heat. Add the plums and sear for 1 minute on each cut side or until golden brown and still firm. Season with a pinch of salt and transfer to a plate; leave the pan over medium-high heat.

Add a splash of olive oil and 1 teaspoon of the coriander seeds to the pan and cook for 15 seconds. Add the sweet potato, season with a little salt and pepper, and sauté, stirring, for 2 minutes. Stir in the orange juice, cover the pan, and cook over medium heat for about 5 minutes or until the sweet potato is soft. Season to taste with salt and pepper, then transfer to a plate. Arrange the seared plums and olives on top, sprinkle with the remaining ½ teaspoon of coriander seeds, and enjoy warm or cold.

SOUPS

Ada's Cold Beet Soup with Cucumber, Radishes, and Egg

SERVES 6

FOR THE SOUP

1½ pounds (680 g) baby beets with their greens (or regular beets plus 2 large chard leaves)

Fine sea salt

1 teaspoon granulated sugar

¾ cup plus 1 tablespoon (200 ml) water

11 ounces (310 g) peeled kirby or Persian cucumbers, coarsely grated

2 cups plus 1 tablespoon (500 ml) buttermilk, cold

1⅔ cups (400 ml) kefir, cold

1¼ cups (300 ml) full-fat plain yogurt, cold

10 medium radishes, trimmed and coarsely grated

2 tablespoons freshly squeezed lemon juice, plus more to taste

1 medium bunch fresh chives, chopped

1 small bunch fresh dill, chopped, reserving a few fronds for the topping

Finely ground pepper

cont'd

Adrianna Jackowska has the talent to make me smile even on my grumpiest days—and so does her Polish cold beet soup. She is the first person who convinced me that cold soup can be great. The soup she grew up with is called chłodnik. It's vibrantly pink, and so crisp, it tastes like biting into a vegetable garden—I find it more refreshing than a salad. Traditionally made in spring or early summer, using baby beets and their tender greens, it's thickened with grated raw cucumber and radishes and topped with fresh dill and chives. The vegetables are stirred into a chilled kefir-buttermilk-yogurt mixture and crowned by a soft-boiled egg. Perfect frugal simplicity. Some add crayfish, which I don't think it needs. Sticking to vegetables and making them shine without distraction is the pure beauty of this soup. And it's quick to prepare: You cook the beets for five minutes and then mix it all together. Ada makes enough for six servings, as it stays fresh in the fridge for a few days, developing just the right depth and flavor on the third day, and is also perfect for inviting friends over.

For the soup, peel the beets and cut into small cubes, then finely chop the beet stems and slice the leaves. Transfer the beets, stems, and leaves to a medium pot and stir in 1 teaspoon of salt, the sugar, and the water. Cover the pot and bring to a boil, then reduce the heat and simmer for 4 to 5 minutes or until al dente. Transfer the beets and cooking liquid to a medium bowl, let cool at room temperature for 10 minutes, and then chill in the fridge until cold.

In a medium bowl, mix the cucumbers with a generous amount of salt and let sit for 15 minutes, then drain and squeeze the cucumber.

cont'd

FOR THE TOPPING

3 to 6 large eggs

18 thin cucumber slices

6 radishes, thinly sliced

Freshly grated lemon zest (optional)

For the topping, place the eggs in a pot, cover with cold water, and bring to a boil. Once the water is boiling, cook for 4 minutes for soft-boiled eggs. Drain the eggs and rinse with cold water. Peel the eggs, set aside, and cut in half lengthwise just before serving.

In a large bowl, whisk together the buttermilk, kefir, and yogurt, then stir in the beets and their cooking liquid, the drained cucumbers, grated radishes, lemon juice, chives, and dill. Season to taste with salt, pepper, and additional lemon juice.

Divide the cold soup among bowls, arrange a few cucumber and radish slices on top, and place a half or a whole egg in the middle. Sprinkle with a little lemon zest and dill and serve immediately. You can keep the soup in the fridge for up to 3 days.

Kale and Sweet Potato Soup with Pasta and Poached Eggs

SERVES 2 TO 3

Olive oil, for sautéing and finishing

1 small onion, cut in half

1 large clove garlic, cut in half

4 ounces (110 g) trimmed kale or cavolo nero leaves, cut into short strips

9 ounces (250 g) peeled sweet potato, cut into small cubes

2½ cups (600 ml) homemade or quality store-bought vegetable broth, hot

6 medium sprigs fresh thyme

2 small sprigs fresh rosemary

2 small bay leaves

Fine sea salt

Finely ground pepper

4 ounces (110 g) pearl-shaped pasta (fregula sarda, orzo pasta, or pearl couscous)

2 to 3 large eggs

This soup is ideal for gray and gloomy days—it's the essence of relaxed cold weather cooking. Made with colorful vegetables, tiny pasta, and poached eggs, it's comforting and will brighten your spirits in less than half an hour. The liquid egg yolk melts into the clear broth, making the soup almost creamy, while the pasta soaks up all the flavors, making it a little richer, more substantial. I like to use fregula sarda, toasted pearl-shaped pasta from Sardinia, which is tender and silky, but orzo or pearl couscous work well, too. Kale and sweet potato are a beautiful duo for a winter soup, but feel free to use white potatoes, parsnip, squash, or canned beans. This recipe welcomes any vegetable that can add subtle sweetness with open arms. You can poach the eggs in the soup, but I prefer to cook them separately.

The vegetables need to cook for about twenty minutes, so check the cooking time of your pasta and add it to the soup early enough that the pasta and vegetables will be done at the same time.

In a medium pot, heat a splash of olive oil over medium heat. Add the onion and garlic and sauté, stirring, for a few minutes or until golden and soft. Add the kale and sweet potato, stir, and cook for 1 minute, then add the hot broth, thyme, rosemary, and bay leaves. Season with salt and pepper and bring to a boil. Reduce the heat, cover, and simmer for 10 minutes. Remove and discard the thyme and rosemary and cook for 10 minutes, adding and cooking the pasta, according to the package instructions, so that the pasta and vegetables will be done at the same time. When the pasta and vegetables are tender, remove and discard the onion, garlic, and bay leaves. Season to taste with salt and pepper, cover, and keep warm.

cont'd

Bring a small saucepan of salted water to a low simmer. Crack 1 egg into a small bowl. Hold a large spoon just over the surface of the water and gently pour the egg onto the spoon. Lower the spoon into the water and hold until the egg white starts to turn white, then use a tablespoon to gently scoop the egg off the large spoon. Poach the egg for 3 minutes. Using a slotted ladle or spoon, transfer the egg to a plate. Poach the remaining eggs the same way, adjusting the heat as needed to maintain a low simmer. You can poach 1 egg at a time or cook all of them together, watching the time for each individual egg.

Divide the soup among bowls and place an egg in the middle of each bowl. Cut the tops of the eggs with a sharp knife and let the egg yolk run into the soup, then drizzle with a little olive oil and serve immediately.

Tomato Soup with Chickpeas and Chèvre

SERVES 2 TO 3

FOR THE SOUP

Olive oil, for sautéing

1 large clove garlic, cut in half

2¼ pounds (1 kg) ripe
tomatoes, roughly chopped

½ cup (120 ml) homemade
or quality store-bought
vegetable broth, hot

1½ tablespoons tomato paste

2 small bay leaves

1 tablespoon balsamic
vinegar, plus more to taste

⅛ teaspoon granulated sugar

Fine sea salt

Finely ground pepper

1 large handful fresh
basil leaves

FOR THE TOPPING

Olive oil, for frying

¾ cup plus 2 tablespoons
(170 g) drained and rinsed
canned chickpeas

⅛ teaspoon fine sea salt

1 teaspoon balsamic vinegar

4 ounces (110 g) aged chèvre
log, cut into thin slices

8 small fresh basil leaves

Coarsely ground pepper

Turn ripe red tomatoes into a soup and you can taste summer on a spoon. The cooking time and the list of ingredients are both quite short here. A little broth, fresh basil, and balsamic vinegar—you really don't need much to make tomatoes shine when they are in the peak of their season. Finishing it off with croutons is popular but something I was never too fond of. I skip the bread and replace it with quickly fried chickpeas. Letting slices of ripe chèvre melt into the puréed soup shifts it from simple to refined. It's divine.

For the soup, heat a splash of olive oil in a large pot over medium-high heat. Add the garlic and sauté, stirring, for 1 minute. Add the tomatoes, bring to a boil, and cook, stirring occasionally, for 4 minutes. Add the hot broth, tomato paste, bay leaves, vinegar, and sugar, stir, and season with a little salt and finely ground pepper. Bring to a boil, then reduce the heat and simmer, uncovered, for 5 minutes. Take the soup off the heat, remove and discard the garlic and bay leaves, and stir in the basil. In a food processor or blender, or with an immersion blender, purée the soup until smooth, then season to taste with additional vinegar, salt, and pepper.

For the topping, heat a splash of olive oil in a small, heavy pan over high heat. Add the chickpeas and salt, immediately cover the pan, as the chickpeas will pop, and fry, shaking the pan occasionally, for about 1 minute or until golden. Take the pan off the heat, stir in the vinegar, and set aside.

Divide the soup among bowls and arrange the chickpeas and chèvre on top. Sprinkle with the basil leaves and a little coarsely ground pepper and serve immediately.

Fifteen-Minute Chicken Soup
with Lime and Vegetables

SERVES 2 TO 3

2½ cups (600 ml) homemade or quality store-bought chicken broth

1½ teaspoons freshly grated lime zest

2 teaspoons freshly squeezed lime juice

2 small bay leaves

Fine sea salt

Finely ground pepper

1 medium boneless, skinless chicken breast

½ medium zucchini, cut into small cubes

⅔ cup (85 g) fresh or frozen peas

2 medium carrots, peeled and thinly sliced

1 celery stalk, thinly sliced

2 teaspoons olive oil

1 spring onion, green part only, sliced

My mother taught me to plunge a whole chicken, lots of vegetables, and fresh herbs in a large pot when cooking a proper chicken soup. It should be rich and concentrated, with shiny drops of golden fat dancing on its surface. And of course, it must cook for at least an hour. So here, we forget about my mother—no offense, Mama—and take a different approach. For my fifteen-minute chicken soup, I'm taking a shortcut. A good store-bought chicken broth—homemade is even better and it freezes so well—infused with lime zest and lime juice is the foundation for cooking a bunch of vegetables and a chicken breast, all at the same time. And once everything is chopped, this only takes fifteen minutes. If you don't like lime, just leave it out or replace it with lemon. I would double the recipe and freeze a portion. It's such a convenient treat when the weather's nasty and you want to warm yourself from within.

In a medium pot, bring the broth, lime zest, lime juice, and bay leaves to a boil and season with salt and pepper. Add the whole chicken breast, zucchini, peas, carrots, and celery, then cover and bring to a low simmer. Make sure to maintain a low simmer, adjusting the heat if necessary; the meat will become tough if the broth is boiling. Cook for 12 to 15 minutes or until the chicken is cooked through; when you cut it in half, it should be white throughout.

Transfer the chicken to a cutting board and, using 2 forks, pull it into bite-size pieces. Season the soup to taste with salt and pepper, then return the chicken to the soup. Stir in the olive oil and spring onion and divide the hot soup among bowls.

Parsnip and Leek Vichyssoise

SERVES 2

Olive oil, for sautéing

4 ounces (110 g) leek (white and green parts), cut into slices

12 ounces (340 g) peeled parsnips, cut into chunky cubes

2½ cups (600 ml) homemade or quality store-bought vegetable broth, hot

2 small bay leaves

Nutmeg, preferably freshly grated

Fine sea salt

Finely ground pepper

2 to 4 teaspoons crème fraîche or sour cream

2 to 4 teaspoons chopped fresh chives

A traditional vichyssoise is made with potatoes, leek, and heavy cream and you're supposed to eat it cold—it's a summer soup. Not following tradition here, we're mixing things up and turning the French classic into a hot and hearty winter treat. Parsnips replace the potatoes, introducing their distinct peppery note to a dish that's usually quite mild. Crème fraîche replaces the cream. It doesn't need much of it, just a tiny dollop, making it creamy but not heavy, with a subtle tangy touch.

In a medium pot, heat a splash of olive oil over medium-high heat. Add the leek and sauté, stirring occasionally, for 2 minutes. Add the parsnips and sauté, stirring, for 2 minutes. Add the hot broth and bay leaves, then season with a little nutmeg, salt, and pepper and bring to a boil. Reduce the heat, cover, and simmer for 15 to 18 minutes or until the parsnips are tender. Remove and discard the bay leaves. In a food processor or blender, or with an immersion blender, purée the soup until smooth, then season to taste with additional nutmeg, salt, and pepper.

Divide the vichyssoise between two bowls. Place a dollop of crème fraîche in the middle of each bowl, sprinkle with chives, and enjoy while hot.

Green Minestrone with Dumplings

SERVES 2

2½ cups (600 ml) homemade or quality store-bought vegetable broth

Fine sea salt

Finely ground pepper

11 ounces (310 g) fresh or frozen mixed green vegetables, such as fava beans, green beans, peas, or small zucchini cubes

1 celery stalk with leaves, thinly sliced

12 ounces (340 g) filled dumplings,* such as Maultaschen, ravioli, or tortellini

It's just a little bowl full of minestrone, but it feels like a hug for the soul. Add some dumplings and you're ready to face whatever the world puts in front of you. I use Maultaschen—large pasta pockets originated in southern Germany and generously filled with minced meat and fresh herbs—that I get from my butcher. Ravioli filled with spinach and ricotta, or tortellini, are just as good. This recipe takes just fifteen minutes to cook and could not be easier: Choose your favorite dumplings, throw them into boiling homemade or store-bought broth to cook with some green vegetables, and you can be sitting in front of a soothing bowl of soup in no time at all.

In a medium pot, bring the broth to a boil and season with a little salt and pepper. Reduce the heat, then add the mixed vegetables and celery and simmer for 10 minutes, adding and cooking the dumplings, according to the package instructions, so that the dumplings and vegetables will be done at the same time; the vegetables should be tender. Season to taste with salt and pepper, then divide between two bowls, sprinkle with the celery leaves, and enjoy warm.

* The vegetables need to cook for about 10 minutes, so check the cooking time of your dumplings and add them to the soup early enough that the dumplings and vegetables will be done at the same time.

Pumpkin Spice Soup with Ginger-Walnut Oil

SERVES 2

FOR THE SOUP

Olive oil, for cooking

About 1¼ inches (3 cm) ginger, cut in half lengthwise

2 small bay leaves

½ teaspoon ground cinnamon, plus more to taste

2½ cups (600 ml) homemade or quality store-bought vegetable broth

14 ounces (400 g) seeded squash, preferably peeled butternut or Hokkaido with skin, cut into cubes

Fine sea salt

Finely ground pepper

FOR THE GINGER-WALNUT OIL

2 tablespoons olive oil

1 teaspoon freshly grated ginger

1 small handful walnuts, roughly chopped

Fine sea salt

A friend gushed over winter squash soup with ginger so much that I had to give it a try. Hooked on the idea of topping it off with toasted walnuts, I decided to also add ground cinnamon, because—with a little imagination—this recipe is like a spiced ginger-walnut cookie turned into soup. It sounds odd, but it tastes great. There's no added sweetness, just the squash, but it's present. The overall result is bright, sharp, and fresh. Thanks to the ginger, it's quite tingly on the tongue. It's definitely spicy and doesn't lose any of its qualities when you freeze it. Just make a fresh batch of the ginger-walnut oil when you pull it out of the freezer.

For the soup, heat a splash of olive oil in a medium pot over medium-high heat. Add the ginger, bay leaves, and cinnamon and cook, stirring constantly, for 30 seconds. Add the broth and bring to a boil. Add the squash, season with salt and pepper, and return to a boil. Reduce the heat, cover, and simmer for about 12 minutes or until the squash is tender. Remove and discard the ginger and bay leaves. In a food processor or blender, or with an immersion blender, purée the soup until smooth, then return it to the pot. Season to taste with salt, pepper, and additional cinnamon, then cover and keep warm. If you prefer to reduce the soup a bit more, bring it to a boil again and cook, stirring constantly, until it reaches the desired taste and texture.

For the ginger-walnut oil, combine the olive oil and ginger in a small saucepan over medium-high heat. Cook, stirring, for about 1 minute or until fragrant and golden. Stir in the walnuts and a pinch of salt and cook for 10 seconds.

Divide the soup between two bowls, drizzle with the ginger-walnut oil, and sprinkle with the walnuts. Enjoy warm!

Quick Fish Soup with Fennel and Dill

SERVES 2 TO 3

4¼ cups (1 L) homemade or quality store-bought fish broth

4 ounces (110 g) cored fennel bulb, sliced

1 celery stalk, thinly sliced

4 grape or cherry tomatoes, cut in half

1 small bunch fresh marjoram

2 small bay leaves

2 slices lemon

1 teaspoon olive oil

1 teaspoon aniseeds or fennel seeds

1 teaspoon fine sea salt

Finely ground pepper

⅛ teaspoon saffron threads (optional)

1 pound (450 g) thick firm fish fillets, such as halibut, cod, or monkfish, cut into 1½ x 1½-inch (4 x 4 cm) chunks

4 fresh mussels, scrubbed and beards cut off

2 medium prawns, peeled and heads removed

1 to 2 tablespoons chopped fresh dill

Fish soup is one of those dishes that people think of as too complicated to cook at home. It isn't. This one only takes twelve minutes and is much easier than cooking fish fillets in a pan. All you need is a good fish broth and firm fish fillets, and then you can play around with fresh herbs and spices. I like to add a few veggies, such as fennel, celery, and tomatoes, which conjure memories of my mother's fish soup. You can add marjoram, bay leaf, aniseed, or some saffron to the broth—just be cautious with saffron, as it's very potent and tends to take over. Anything that pulls the soup in a licoricey direction is also great: pastis, the French anise-flavored spirit, fennel seeds, or a vermouth, such as Noilly Prat. And fresh dill, of course.

In a large pot, bring the broth to a boil, then add the fennel, celery, tomatoes, marjoram, bay leaves, lemon slices, olive oil, aniseeds, salt, a little pepper, and the saffron. Reduce the heat and simmer, uncovered, for 5 minutes. Add the fish, mussels, and prawns, then reduce the heat to medium-low, keeping it just below simmering. Cover, and poach for 5 to 7 minutes or until the fish is just cooked through and you can flake it with a fork. Remove and discard the marjoram, bay leaves, and lemon slices and season to taste with salt and pepper. Divide the soup among bowls, sprinkle with dill, and enjoy hot.

Cauliflower Soup with Tahini and Sourdough Croutons

SERVES 2

2 ounces (60 g) white sourdough bread with crust, cut into ¾-inch (2 cm) cubes

2 teaspoons olive oil, plus more for finishing

2½ cups (600 ml) homemade or quality store-bought vegetable broth

2 long strips fresh lemon peel (white pith removed)

1 to 1½ tablespoons freshly squeezed lemon juice

2 small bay leaves

Nutmeg, preferably freshly grated

Fine sea salt

Finely ground pepper

11 ounces (310 g) cored cauliflower, cut into florets

1½ to 2 tablespoons light tahini

10 fresh flat-leaf parsley leaves, for serving

1½ to 2 teaspoons freshly grated lemon zest, for serving

Cauliflower and tahini are a great match, especially in a puréed soup. Let a generous squeeze of lemon join the nutty sesame sauce and together they will enliven the cauliflower. Instead of drifting into blandness, the soup has depth and an assertive oomph. Chunky cubes of sourdough bread, briefly seared in a very hot pan, bring a smoky touch and scrumptious crunch. Sometimes it's so easy to turn a simple vegetable soup into an exciting lunch.

On a large plate, drizzle the bread cubes with the 2 teaspoons of olive oil. Heat a medium, heavy pan over high heat, without adding any fat, until the pan is very hot. Add the bread cubes and toast, turning them constantly, for 1½ to 2 minutes or until crunchy and golden brown with a few dark freckles. Transfer the bread to a plate.

In a medium pot, bring the broth, lemon peel, 1 tablespoon of the lemon juice, and the bay leaves to a boil and season with a little nutmeg, salt, and pepper. Add the cauliflower, then reduce the heat, cover, and simmer for about 10 minutes or until the cauliflower is tender. Remove and discard the bay leaves and lemon peel. Use a slotted ladle or spoon to remove a few cauliflower florets, then break or cut them into bite-size pieces and set aside for serving. Add 1½ tablespoons of the tahini to the soup. In a food processor or blender, or with an immersion blender, purée the soup until smooth. Season to taste with additional tahini, lemon juice, nutmeg, salt, and pepper.

Divide the warm soup and the reserved cauliflower florets between two bowls. Arrange the toasted bread cubes on top, sprinkle with the parsley and lemon zest, and drizzle with a few drops of olive oil.

Butter Bean and Fennel Soup with Crispy Bacon

SERVES 2

Olive oil, for sautéing and finishing

1 large clove garlic

2½ cups (600 ml) homemade or quality store-bought vegetable broth

2 small bay leaves

Nutmeg, preferably freshly grated

Fine sea salt

Finely ground pepper

6 ounces (170 g) cored fennel bulb, roughly chopped, plus a few chopped fronds for the topping

1¼ cups (250 g) drained and rinsed canned butter (lima) or cannellini beans

2 slices bacon

2 teaspoons crème fraîche or sour cream

Butter beans and fennel complement each other like good old friends—they share similarities yet have their own unique qualities. Cooked, they are both quite mild, not overpowering, but their textures couldn't be further apart. While the beans become soft, the fennel stays fibrous and keeps its texture, which is nice, especially in a puréed soup. This recipe isn't adventurous but harmonious—it's a true soul pleaser. You can cream it up with a dollop of crème fraîche or top it off with a crispy slice of bacon. If you want your toppings to stay on top, and not drown, you should reduce and thicken the soup a little once you've puréed it.

In a medium pot, heat a splash of olive oil over medium-high heat. Add the whole garlic clove and sauté, stirring, for 1 minute. Add the broth and bay leaves, season with a little nutmeg, salt, and pepper, and bring to a boil. Add the fennel bulb, then cover the pot, reduce the heat, and simmer for 10 minutes or until tender. Add the butter beans and cook for 2 minutes. Remove and discard the garlic and bay leaves. In a food processor or blender, or with an immersion blender, purée the soup until smooth, then return it to the pot. If the soup is too thin, bring it to a boil, then lower the heat to medium-high and reduce, stirring constantly, until it starts to thicken or reaches the desired texture. Season to taste with additional nutmeg, salt, and pepper, cover, and keep warm.

In a medium, heavy pan, heat a small splash of olive oil over medium-high heat and cook the bacon, turning occasionally, for a few minutes or until golden brown and crispy. Transfer the bacon to a plate, let cool for 1 minute, and break into large pieces.

Divide the soup between two bowls, top with the crème fraîche and bacon, and sprinkle with a few fennel fronds and pepper. Drizzle each portion with 1 teaspoon of olive oil and enjoy hot.

SANDWICHES

Turmeric Apricot and Ricotta Sandwich

MAKES 2 SANDWICHES

FOR THE RICOTTA

6 ounces (170 g) fresh ricotta

1 teaspoon freshly squeezed orange juice

⅓ to ½ teaspoon ground turmeric

Fine sea salt

FOR THE SANDWICHES

1 tablespoon honey

¼ teaspoon ground turmeric

4 medium apricots, pitted and cut in half

1 medium loaf ciabatta, cut into 2 buns and each cut in half

8 fresh basil leaves

When apricot and turmeric meet in a sandwich it resembles a late summer sunset in the Mediterranean, seconds before the sun drops into the sea—they share the same warm golden hue. The flavors of the two are both assertive, stirring up the dish and adding excitement. We use the turmeric to spice up seared apricots, sweetened with a little honey, and to brighten creamy ricotta. When you layer the smooth dip and juicy fruit on soft ciabatta and add a few fresh basil leaves, you can be assured that noon will be far from dull.

For the ricotta, whisk together the ricotta, orange juice, and ⅓ teaspoon of turmeric in a medium bowl. Season to taste with salt and additional turmeric and set aside.

For the sandwiches, melt the honey and turmeric in a small, heavy pan over high heat until bubbly. Add the apricots, skin-side up, and sear for 1 minute or until golden brown; reduce the heat if they brown too quickly. Flip the apricots and sear for about 1 minute or until they start to soften but still hold their shape. Remove the pan from the heat and set aside.

Spread the ricotta on the bottom halves of the ciabatta buns, arrange the apricots on top, and drizzle with the cooking juices from the pan. Sprinkle with the basil and place a top on each bun or enjoy as an open sandwich.

Sauerkraut and Hummus on Sourdough Bread

MAKES 1 LARGE SANDWICH

FOR THE HUMMUS*

1¼ cups (250 g) drained and rinsed canned chickpeas

⅔ cup (150 g) light tahini

⅓ cup (75 ml) water

¼ cup (60 ml) freshly squeezed lemon juice

1 large clove garlic, crushed

2 whole cloves, finely crushed with a mortar and pestle

¾ teaspoon ground cinnamon

½ teaspoon fine sea salt

¼ teaspoon ground cumin

FOR THE SANDWICH

1 large slice thickly cut spelt or rye bread, ideally sourdough

2 to 3 tablespoons drained jarred or canned sauerkraut

Sauerkraut and hummus seems like the weirdest combination, but it's genius. It's so good that I couldn't believe it and had to turn to my friend Laurel Kratochvila of Fine Bagels in Berlin for consultation: "Hummus and sauerkraut? I've never had it before, but it makes sense—a good hit of acid!" Go for dark bread—the richness of the dip and the fermented cabbage's acidity need a hearty carb base. All the ingredients are kitchen staples. You can even use your favorite hummus from the market, but in case you prefer to make your own, I'm including the recipe for my spiced hummus.

For the hummus, purée the chickpeas, tahini, water, lemon juice, garlic, cloves, cinnamon, salt, and cumin in a food processor or blender until smooth. Season to taste with additional salt and transfer to a small bowl.

For the sandwich, generously spread 2 to 3 tablespoons of the hummus on the bread, pile the sauerkraut on top, and enjoy!

* You can use leftover hummus for other recipes, such as Roasted Eggplant and Hummus on Dark Bread with an Herb-Fried Egg (page 138).

Roasted Eggplant and Hummus
on Dark Bread with an Herb-Fried Egg

MAKES 1 SANDWICH

FOR THE EGGPLANT

1 medium eggplant, cut lengthwise into ¼-inch-thick (0.5 cm) slices

Olive oil, for broiling

Flaky sea salt

Coarsely ground pepper

FOR THE SANDWICH

1 teaspoon unsalted butter

1 large egg

6 fresh herb leaves, such as parsley, dill, or basil

Flaky sea salt

Coarsely ground pepper

2 to 3 tablespoons hummus (page 137 or store-bought)

1 slice spelt or rye bread

Roasted eggplant, hummus, and egg is a trusted sandwich combination that will never let you down. It's sweet, smooth, and rich, with soft layers that literally melt in your mouth. For this popular sabich sandwich, which was brought to Israel by Iraqi Jews, the egg can be poached or hard-boiled. Or we can take a different approach, frying the egg and decorating it with fresh herbs. You can use hummus from the market, or make your own (page 137), which only takes a few minutes if you use canned chickpeas. Roasting the eggplant requires twenty minutes and the recipe makes more than you need, so you may want to prepare that ahead and keep it in the fridge to use for pasta or for other sandwiches (page 157).

Set the oven to broil (quicker method) or preheat to 500°F (260°C).

For the eggplant, set a wire rack on a rimmed baking sheet and arrange the eggplant slices, side by side, on the rack. Brush both sides of the eggplant slices with olive oil and season just the top with salt and pepper. Broil the eggplant, turning once, for 5 to 7 minutes per side, or roast at 500°F (260°C) for 15 minutes, then flip and continue roasting for about 6 minutes. The eggplant should be golden and partly brown but not black. Stack the eggplant slices on a plate and let them sit for at least 2 minutes; you can use them warm or cold.

For the sandwich, heat the butter in a small, heavy pan over medium-high heat. When it's sizzling, crack the egg into the pan, arrange the herbs on top of the egg white, and cook for 2 to 3 minutes or until the egg white is just set and the yolk is still runny. Season to taste with salt and pepper.

Spread the hummus on the bread, arrange 2 slices of eggplant on top, and finish with the fried egg—enjoy while the egg is still warm!

Grilled Raclette and Fennel Melt Sandwich

MAKES 1 LARGE SANDWICH

Olive oil, for cooking

6 ounces (170 g) cored fennel bulb, cut into very thin slices

Fine sea salt

Coarsely ground pepper

3 ounces (85 g) Raclette (or Comté or Gruyère), coarsely grated

2 large slices white sourdough bread, ⅓ to ½ inch (0.75 to 1.25 cm) thick

1½ tablespoons unsalted butter

I was introduced to the concept of a melt sandwich quite late in my life. It all started with a tuna melt in New York City. While a tuna sandwich wasn't new to me—it's something my mother often made when I was a child—adding cheese was strange to my German palate and I found it confusing at first. However, I was hooked after the first bite and immediately started thinking about fillings beyond tuna, such as fennel. Cooking very thinly sliced fennel bulb in a skillet until it almost resembles caramelized onions does something interesting to this vegetable. Its licoricey note fades into the background and a sweet-smoky taste emerges instead. For the cheese to keep up, I recommend using a strong one. Raclette is a perfect choice, but Comté or Gruyère is also assertive enough for this melted cheese treat.

In a medium, heavy pan, heat a splash of olive oil over medium-high heat. Add the fennel, season with salt and pepper, and cook, stirring occasionally and reducing the heat if it browns too quickly, for 13 to 15 minutes or until golden brown and very soft. Transfer the fennel to a medium bowl, then wipe out the pan with a paper towel and set aside.

Add the cheese to the warm fennel and mix to combine. Immediately spread the fennel-cheese mixture on a slice of bread and cover with the second slice of bread, pressing down gently.

Add 1 tablespoon of the butter to the pan used to cook the fennel and melt over medium-high heat. As soon as it's sizzling, add the sandwich, reduce the heat to medium, and cook for about 4 minutes or until the bottom is golden brown and crunchy. Add the remaining ½ tablespoon of butter, then flip the sandwich, gently pressing it down for a few seconds, and cook for about 4 minutes or until the bottom is golden brown and the cheese has melted. Transfer the sandwich to a plate, cut it in half, and sprinkle with a little pepper. Enjoy while the cheese is hot!

Tzatziki Bun with Seared Radishes

MAKES 2 SANDWICHES

1 cup (230 g) full-fat plain
Greek yogurt (or 1 cup / 230 g
quark whisked with 2 tablespoons heavy cream)

7 ounces (200 g) peeled
cucumber, coarsely grated,
drained, and firmly squeezed,
plus 8 cucumber slices
with skin

2 teaspoons finely chopped
fresh mint leaves, plus more
to taste

Fine sea salt

Finely ground pepper

Olive oil, for searing

10 radishes, cut in half

2 spelt or rye buns, cut in half

It's not authentic, but I prefer to make tzatziki with quark and a dash of heavy cream rather than using yogurt. However, quark is hard to find in many countries, so Greek yogurt is the easier choice. For lunch, I keep my tzatziki garlic-free and stir in chopped fresh mint. Raw radishes would make a crisp spring topping, but if you sear them briefly, their spicy, peppery note slightly softens and so does their texture. Just choose according to your mood. You can use leftover tzatziki for more sandwiches or as a dip for boiled potatoes; just keep it covered in the fridge for up to two days.

In a medium bowl, whisk together the yogurt, grated cucumber, and mint and season to taste with salt, pepper, and additional mint; you want the mint to be present but not overpowering. Set the tzatzki aside.

In a small, heavy pan, heat a small splash of olive oil over high heat. Sear the radishes, turning once, for 1 to 2 minutes or until golden with a few dark freckles. Season with a little salt, transfer to a plate, and let cool for a few minutes.

Divide the cucumber slices between the bottom halves of the buns and spread a generous amount of tzatziki on top. Arrange the radishes on top of the tzatziki, place the tops on the buns, and enjoy. It will be messy.

Beet Cream Cheese and Smoked Fish on a Bun

MAKES 1 SANDWICH

1 large beet, scrubbed

1 bay leaf

2 tablespoons cream cheese (or ricotta or sour cream)

2 teaspoons freshly squeezed lemon juice

1 teaspoon olive oil (optional)

Fine sea salt

Finely ground pepper

1 spelt or rye bun, cut in half

2 ounces (60 g) smoked trout fillet

1 teaspoon capers

Pink beet, cream cheese, and pale smoked fish make for a stunner of a sandwich. Sweet and smoky, silky and smooth—it just needs something a little sour or salty to make it complete. You could sneak in pickled gherkins, but salty capers are also thrilling. A dark rye or spelt bun is ideal, as it's a little heartier than wheat and won't vanish under these strong toppings. I even like to go for a crunchy Vinschgauer, a mountain bun popular in the Alps, that is spiced with coriander, fennel, and caraway seeds. Choosing the right fish is easy: You don't want anything fancy. Smoked trout is both frugal and delicate and easily finds its place on top of the puréed beet and cream cheese spread. This freshwater fish balances sweet and earthy and is not as fatty and dominating as smoked salmon or eel— but take your pick. You can even leave out the fish to make an equally delicious vegetarian sandwich. And if you happen to already have boiled beet lying around, you will save some time when you prepare the dip.

Bring a medium pot of salted water to a boil. Add the beet and bay leaf, then reduce the heat, cover, and simmer for 45 to 50 minutes or until tender. Drain the beet, rinse with cold water, and let cool completely before peeling.

Cut 2 slices from the middle of the beet and set aside. In a blender or food processor, combine the remaining beet (about 3 ounces / 85 g), cream cheese, and lemon juice and purée until smooth. If the dip is too firm, stir in the olive oil. Season to taste with salt and pepper.

Place the beet slices on the bottom half of the bun, cover with the beet cream cheese (you might not need all of it), and arrange the fish fillet on top. Sprinkle with the capers, place the top on the bun, and enjoy immediately.

Torta al Testo with Caprese

MAKES 6 SANDWICHES

FOR THE FLATBREAD

2 cups (260 g) all-purpose flour

3 teaspoons fast-acting yeast

¼ teaspoon fine sea salt

⅔ cup (150 ml) water, lukewarm

FOR THE SANDWICHES

9 ounces (250 g) mozzarella, drained and cut into small cubes

24 grape or cherry tomatoes, cut in half

1 handful fresh basil leaves

Olive oil, for drizzling

Balsamic vinegar, for drizzling

Fine sea salt

Finely ground pepper

Torta al testo is a traditional Umbrian flatbread. Imagine little pockets of dough, shaped to be filled with summery vegetables, raw or grilled, and mozzarella, ricotta, or—crossing borders—Greek feta. Thanks to fast-acting yeast, it's a quick dough to make and it's baked in a hot skillet on the stove for just three minutes. Baking bread in a hot, smoking pan feels very archaic, and tearing a piece of the warm blistered bread feels utterly satisfying. It's one of my favorite recipes to treat myself to or to serve as a starter for a casual Saturday lunch or dinner with friends. Both a Caprese salad and a Greek salad embody the essence of Mediterranean food and make a perfect torta al testo filling. I can't even say which I prefer.

For the flatbread, combine the flour, yeast, and salt in the bowl of a stand mixer fitted with the dough hook attachment. Add the lukewarm water and mix with the dough hook for about 3 minutes or until well combined and smooth. On a work surface, continue kneading with your hands for 2 minutes or until you have a soft and silky ball of dough. Place the dough back in the bowl, cover with a tea towel, and let rise in a warm place for 20 minutes or until almost doubled in size (at room temperature during summer and on the heater or in the warm oven during winter).

Take the dough out of the bowl and divide it into 6 equal parts. On a floured work surface, use a rolling pin to roll each piece into a 4-inch (10 cm) disc. Cover the discs with a tea towel and let them rise on the work surface for 15 to 20 minutes or until puffy.

cont'd

Heat a large cast-iron pan over high heat, without adding any fat, until the pan is very hot. Working in batches, arrange 2 to 3 discs of dough in the pan and cook, flipping once and reducing the heat as necessary, for 45 seconds to 1½ minutes per side or until golden brown, puffed up, and baked through. Watch the flatbreads closely so that they don't burn. Repeat to bake the remaining flatbreads and let cool for a few minutes.

For the sandwiches, cut each warm flatbread in half like a bun without cutting all the way through; they should be like pockets, open on one side. Divide the mozzarella, tomatoes, and basil among the flatbreads, drizzle with a little olive oil and vinegar, and season to taste with salt and pepper. Enjoy immediately!

Torta al Testo with Greek Salad

MAKES 6 SANDWICHES

6 flatbreads (page 147)

5 ounces (140 g) feta,
cut into cubes

18 grape or cherry
tomatoes, cut in half

12 small radishes, cut in half

½ large cucumber, scrubbed,
cut in half lengthwise,
and cut into 24 slices

⅓ celery stalk, thinly sliced

1 small handful flat-leaf
parsley leaves

Olive oil, for drizzling

White balsamic vinegar
(or freshly squeezed lemon
juice), for drizzling

Flaky sea salt

Coarsely ground pepper

Cut each warm flatbread in half like a bun without cutting all the way through; they should be like pockets, open on one side. Divide the feta, tomatoes, radishes, cucumber, celery, and parsley among the flatbreads, drizzle with a little olive oil and vinegar, and season to taste with salt and pepper. The flatbread tastes best when you eat it immediately after filling, so don't let it sit for too long.

Ciabatta with Balsamic Blackberries, Coppa di Parma, and Mustard

MAKES 2 SANDWICHES

4 ounces (110 g) fresh blackberries

1 teaspoon balsamic vinegar

⅛ teaspoon fine sea salt

8 very thin slices coppa di Parma or 4 slices prosciutto di Parma

1 medium loaf ciabatta, cut into 2 buns and each cut in half

2 to 4 teaspoons Dijon mustard

In my second cookbook, *365: A Year of Everyday Cooking and Baking*, I included a recipe for roasted pork fillet wrapped in melted blackberries, mustard, and coppa di Parma. It's a gorgeous combo, covering the range from sweet to salty to spicy. For a while, I pondered over ways to transform this hearty pleasure into a quick sandwich. The solution was easier than expected: I just left out the pork fillet and layered the ingredients on crusty ciabatta. The blackberries are seared over high heat and deglazed with balsamic vinegar, enhancing their sweet and tart taste, which means you can even use berries that aren't at the peak—the heat will take care of them.

Heat a small, heavy pan over high heat, not adding any fat. When the pan is hot, add the blackberries and sear, shaking the pan and gently stirring, for 1 minute. Stir in the vinegar and salt and cook for about 1 minute or until the blackberries start to soften but still hold their shape; mind that they don't burn. Take the pan off the heat and set aside.

Divide the coppa di Parma between the bottom halves of the buns and arrange the warm blackberries on top; you can also prepare the blackberries in advance and briefly warm them up. Drizzle the berries with the mustard and place a top on each bun—or enjoy as an open sandwich, which is less messy.

Squash Pesto Sandwich with Feta and Date

MAKES 1 SANDWICH

FOR THE PESTO*

8 ounces (225 g) seeded and peeled squash, preferably butternut or Hokkaido, cut into 1-inch (2.5 cm) wedges

1 tablespoon olive oil

Flaky sea salt

2 tablespoons freshly squeezed orange juice

1 tablespoon unsalted cashews

⅛ teaspoon ground cumin (optional)

FOR THE SANDWICH

1 spelt or rye bun, cut in half

1 ounce (30 g) feta, crumbled

1 large soft, juicy date, cut in half lengthwise, pitted, and cut into long strips

My definition of pesto is quite flexible. Italians would roll their eyes, but in my kitchen, anything my blender can purée and that goes well with pasta and sandwiches earns the pesto name. Even the word *pesto* gets me excited about a recipe, making me think of la dolce vita and Tuscan holidays. Take, for example, roasted squash pesto. Calling it a purée wouldn't do it any justice and would only limit the fun, especially if we add crumbled feta and a juicy date to a sandwich that spans the spectrum of hearty, sweet, and tart with such ease. You can roast double the amount of squash from the start and also use it for salads (pages 28 and 31).

Preheat the oven to 400°F (200°C).

For the pesto, place the squash in a medium baking dish, drizzle with the olive oil, and toss to coat. Arrange the squash side by side, sprinkle with a little salt, and roast for 30 minutes or until soft. Transfer the squash to a food processor or blender, add the orange juice, cashews, and cumin, and purée until smooth. Let cool for at least 10 minutes.

For the sandwich, generously spread the pesto on the bottom half of the bun, arrange the feta and date on top, and place the top on the bun. Enjoy.

* You can use leftover pesto for pasta.

Camembert Baguette with Quick Peach–Basil Chutney

MAKES 2 SANDWICHES

1 large white doughnut peach

1 large yellow peach

15 large fresh basil leaves, very thinly sliced, plus 10 small leaves for serving

1½ teaspoons olive oil

1½ teaspoons balsamic vinegar, plus more to taste

½ teaspoon Dijon mustard, plus more to taste

⅛ teaspoon fine sea salt

6 ounces (170 g) aged Camembert or Brie de Meaux, thickly sliced

1 slim, long baguette, cut into 2 large buns and each cut in half

When I go on a bike tour to one of the lakes outside Berlin, I often pack half a baguette filled with ripe Camembert and drizzled with fig mustard. It makes a pretty good picnic. You don't need to bother with any weak components—the mature French cheese would overpower them. Ripe fruit, especially peaches, and Dijon mustard are perfect. If you invest ten minutes, and add vinegar and basil, you can even have a quick chutney. The stone fruit is cooked in boiling water for a few minutes, which softens the pulp and makes it easier to peel. Then you'll only need to chop and season it and your chutney is ready for a bike tour.

Bring a small pot of water to a boil and blanch the peaches for 4 to 7 minutes or until you can easily peel off their skins; mind that the cooking time depends on their ripeness. Drain the peaches and, using a knife or your fingers, peel off their skins under running cold water. Transfer the peaches to a cutting board, cut in half, and remove the pits. Chop the peaches roughly, then transfer to a medium bowl and mix with the sliced basil.

In a small bowl, whisk together the olive oil, vinegar, mustard, and salt and add to the peaches. Gently mix and season to taste with additional vinegar and mustard; mind that the vinegar and mustard aren't too overpowering.

Divide the Camembert between the bottom halves of the baguette buns, scoop the peach chutney on top of the cheese, and sprinkle with the basil leaves. Cover the buns with their tops—or enjoy as open sandwiches.

Roasted Eggplant and Bacon Sandwich
with Butter Bean–Basil Pesto

MAKES 2 TO 3 SANDWICHES

FOR THE SANDWICHES

1 medium eggplant (about
9 ounces / 250 g), cut into
½-inch-thick (1.25 cm) circles

¼ cup (60 ml) olive oil,
plus more for cooking

Flaky sea salt

Coarsely ground pepper

2 to 3 slices bacon

2 to 3 spelt or rye buns,
cut in half

FOR THE PESTO

1¼ cups (250 g) drained and
rinsed canned butter beans
(lima beans; or cannellini
beans)

2 tablespoons olive oil

1 handful fresh basil leaves,
plus a few small leaves
for serving

Fine sea salt

Coarsely ground pepper

You could call this thick butter bean–basil pesto "puréed beans," but that wouldn't sound as tempting. This unusual pesto is similar to hummus yet lighter and fresher. It doesn't need much olive oil but requires a full handful of fragrant basil leaves. It's another one of these startling pantry wonders—we have all the ingredients lying around most of the time but don't know what to do with them. You can keep the pesto in the fridge for days and use it as a spread on toasted bread or stir it into warm pasta (page 191). Layering it with roasted eggplant slices leads to a luscious sandwich. Crispy bacon adds salty crunch and increases the fun, but it's just as good when you keep it meat-free. If you're looking for other combinations, try pairing the eggplant with hummus (page 138).

Preheat the oven to 425°F (220°C).

For the sandwiches, toss the eggplant and the ¼ cup (60 ml) of olive oil in a medium baking dish. Arrange the eggplant slices side by side and season with flaky sea salt and pepper. Roast for 20 minutes, then flip the eggplant slices and continue roasting for 10 minutes or until golden brown and soft; mind that they don't burn.

Meanwhile, for the pesto, purée the butter beans, olive oil, and basil in a food processor or blender until smooth. Season to taste with fine sea salt and pepper.

In a medium, heavy pan, heat a small splash of olive oil over medium-high heat and cook the bacon, turning occasionally, for a few minutes or until golden brown and crispy.

Layer the warm or cold roasted eggplant slices and the butter bean–basil pesto on the bottom halves of the buns. Place the bacon on top and sprinkle with basil leaves and pepper, then place a top on each bun and enjoy.

Apple and Taleggio in Carrozza Sandwich

MAKES 2 SANDWICHES

2½ tablespoons unsalted butter

1 teaspoon coriander seeds, crushed with a mortar and pestle

1 medium, sour apple, cored and sliced

3 tablespoons whole milk

1 large egg

⅛ teaspoon fine sea salt

2 tablespoons all-purpose flour

4 slices soft white bread

2 ounces (60 g) Taleggio, fontina, or Robiola, coarsely grated

Coarsely ground pepper

An in carrozza—which translates to "in a carriage"—is like a savory French toast and usually filled with mozzarella. Italians love this frugal snack. You only need soft white bread, eggs, and milk, but when it comes to the filling, you can go wild. Don't be bound by the classic version, which uses only mozzarella. Spices, fruit, sautéed vegetables, and aromatic cheese work well and introduce a little more excitement. Both apple and Taleggio have a fruity taste and complement each other in this recipe. For more complexity, sneak in crushed coriander seeds and let their citrusy notes unfold.

In a medium, heavy pan, heat 1 tablespoon of the butter over medium-high heat until it sizzles, then add the coriander seeds and cook for 10 seconds. Add the apple slices and cook for 1 minute per side or until golden brown and still firm. Transfer the apple and coriander seeds to a plate and set the pan aside.

In a shallow bowl, whisk together the milk, egg, and salt. Spread the flour on a flat plate.

Divide the apple slices and coriander seeds between 2 slices of bread, leaving a thin border around the edges. Arrange the cheese on top, cover with a second slice of bread, and press the sandwiches together. Dip both sides of the sandwiches in the flour until lightly coated, then gently dip the sandwiches in the egg-milk mixture, flipping and continuing to dip until all the liquid is soaked up.

In the pan used to cook the apple, heat the remaining 1½ tablespoons of butter over medium-high heat. Add the sandwiches and cook for a few minutes or until golden brown and crispy. Flip the sandwiches over and cook for 1 to 2 minutes or until golden brown and the cheese is melted, reducing the heat to medium if they brown too quickly. Cut the sandwiches in half diagonally, sprinkle with a little pepper, and enjoy immediately.

Ciabatta Sandwich with Roquefort Omelet and Seared Plums

MAKES 2 SANDWICHES

2 large dark plums, pitted and cut into quarters

1 teaspoon balsamic vinegar

Fine sea salt

3 large eggs

¼ cup (60 ml) heavy cream

Nutmeg, preferably freshly grated

Finely ground pepper

1 teaspoon unsalted butter

1 ounce (30 g) Roquefort or Stilton, cut into small cubes

4 small romaine lettuce leaves

1 medium loaf ciabatta, cut into 2 buns and each cut in half

A blue cheese omelet with dark plums is a glorious combination, so good that I wouldn't even consider using another fruit. Seared only for seconds in a scorching hot pan, then deglazed with balsamic vinegar, the plums add depth and lushness to a classic egg sandwich. Roquefort—Stilton would also be fine—ensures that the omelet is potent enough for this enchanting encounter with fruit. It's messy to eat, but who cares when it tastes so good?

Heat a small, heavy pan over high heat, without adding any fat, until the pan is very hot. Add the plums, cut-side down, and sear for 10 to 15 seconds or until golden brown. Quickly flip the plums and sear on the other cut side for 10 to 15 seconds or until golden brown. Add the vinegar and a pinch of salt, stir, and then immediately take the pan off the heat and set aside.

In a medium bowl, whisk together the eggs and heavy cream and season with nutmeg, salt, and pepper.

In a small cast-iron pan or nonstick skillet, heat the butter over medium-high heat. Pour the egg mixture into the pan and stir 3 to 4 times. Be careful to not scramble the eggs and to just fluff them up a bit; reduce the heat if they brown too quickly. When the bottom side is golden, flip the omelet and cook the other side for 1 to 2 minutes or until golden and just set. Take the pan off the heat and sprinkle the Roquefort over the omelet. Cut the omelet in half and layer the halves on top of each other so that the cheese can melt in the middle, then gently cut the omelet in half again.

Divide the lettuce leaves between the bottom halves of the buns and place the warm omelet on top. Arrange the plums on top of the omelet, then place a top on each bun. Squeeze a little and enjoy—it will be messy.

Egg Sandwich with Artichoke, Tomato, and Pesto

MAKES 2 SANDWICHES

FOR THE PESTO

¼ cup (60 ml) olive oil

1 ounce (30 g) fresh
basil leaves

2 tablespoons finely
grated Parmesan

1 tablespoon pine nuts
or cashews

1 small clove garlic (optional)

Fine sea salt

FOR THE SANDWICHES

3 large eggs

¼ cup (60 ml) heavy cream

Nutmeg, preferably
freshly grated

Fine sea salt

Finely ground pepper

Olive oil, for cooking

3 artichoke hearts, marinated
in olive oil, drained, and cut
in half lengthwise

1 teaspoon unsalted butter

8 large fresh basil leaves

1 medium loaf ciabatta, cut
into 2 buns and each
cut in half

3 grape or cherry tomatoes,
cut in half

Marinated artichoke hearts add a sweet and briny taste—and excitement—to a frugal egg sandwich. It's a summer omelet, inviting the cook to be playful. Tiny tomatoes and green pesto—homemade is always better, but store-bought pesto also works—make it fresh and juicy. As an alternative, you could also think of a Greek salad and top the warm egg with crumbled feta, cucumber, and olives. No matter what sparks your imagination, you can easily keep it vegetarian; this sandwich doesn't really need meat.

For the pesto, purée the olive oil, basil, Parmesan, pine nuts, and garlic in a food processor or blender until smooth and season to taste with salt.

For the sandwiches, whisk together the eggs and heavy cream in a medium bowl, season with nutmeg, salt, and pepper, and set aside.

In a small cast-iron pan or nonstick skillet, heat a small splash of olive oil over medium-high heat. Add the artichoke hearts and cook, turning once, for 1 minute or until golden and a little crispy. Transfer to a plate, but leave the pan on the heat.

Heat the butter in the pan over medium-high heat. When it's sizzling, pour in the egg mixture and stir 3 to 4 times. Be careful not to scramble the eggs and to just fluff them up a bit; reduce the heat if they brown too quickly. When the bottom side is golden, flip the omelet and cook the other side for 1 to 2 minutes or until golden and just set. Take the pan off the heat and cut the omelet in half.

Divide the basil leaves between the bottom halves of the buns, drizzle with a little pesto, and place the omelet halves on top. Arrange the artichoke hearts and tomatoes on top of the omelet, drizzle with more pesto, and place a top on each bun. Squeeze and enjoy!

Roasted Coriander Cauliflower, Tomato, and Tahini on Sourdough

1 pound (450 g) medium cauliflower florets, cut in half lengthwise

3 tablespoons olive oil, plus more for brushing

1 tablespoon coriander seeds, crushed with a mortar and pestle

Flaky sea salt

Coarsely ground pepper

¼ cup (60 g) light tahini

¼ cup (60 ml) water

⅛ teaspoon fine sea salt

4 large slices thickly cut white sourdough bread (or any crusty white bread)

2 to 4 tablespoons tomato paste

Piling roasted cauliflower on a slice of sourdough bread was more of a spontaneous move than a premeditated idea. I'd already spread tomato paste on a crusty slice of bread brushed with olive oil—a classic in the Mediterranean—when I remembered the leftover cauliflower I had roasted the night before. I grabbed a few florets, drizzled them with tahini, and I was hooked. The cauliflower, showered with a generous amount of crushed coriander seeds, adds a floral, lemony note. There's a lot happening in this sandwich, but not too much. If you don't feel like wolfing down four sandwiches, just keep leftover cauliflower in the fridge for up to two days and use it for salads.

Preheat the oven to 425°F (220°C).

Spread the cauliflower in a medium baking dish, drizzle with the 3 tablespoons of olive oil, and sprinkle with the coriander seeds and a little flaky sea salt and pepper. Using your hands, gently mix the cauliflower, then arrange the florets side by side and roast for 22 to 25 minutes or until golden brown and tender. You can switch on the broiler for about 1 minute if you prefer the cauliflower a little darker.

In a small bowl, whisk together the tahini, water, and fine sea salt.

Brush each slice of bread with 1 to 2 teaspoons of olive oil and 1 to 2 teaspoons of tomato paste. Divide the warm or cold cauliflower and coriander seeds among the slices of bread, drizzle with the tahini sauce, and season to taste with flaky sea salt and pepper. Enjoy!

Baguette with Roasted Grapes, Burrata, and Prosciutto di Parma

MAKES 2 SANDWICHES

8 ounces (225 g) seedless red grapes, on the vine

1 tablespoon olive oil, plus more for drizzling

Flaky sea salt

6 very thin slices prosciutto di Parma (or prosciutto di San Daniele)

⅓ baguette, cut into 2 buns and each cut in half

4 ounces (110 g) burrata (or mozzarella di bufala), drained and torn in half

A few fresh basil leaves

Coarsely ground pepper

This is the most sensual sandwich in the world. It's lush and juicy, opulent but not pretentious. Red grapes on the vine are roasted for half an hour until they start to shrivel and shrink. They don't need to be warm, so you can prepare them in advance. The heat concentrates their flavors, emphasizing their natural sweetness. If you're already hooked, double the recipe and use them as a topping for salad (page 28). For this sandwich, they are gracefully added to creamy burrata and delicate prosciutto di Parma. It's a sandwich of your dreams— or my dreams, at least. You could even skip the baguette and turn this into an unconventional variation on caprese.

Preheat the oven to 425°F (220°C).

Place the grapes (on the vine) in a medium baking dish, then drizzle with the 1 tablespoon of olive oil, gently toss to coat, and season with a little salt. Roast for about 30 minutes or until the grapes are soft and a little shriveled. Let the grapes cool for a few minutes, or let cool completely, and either snip them off the vine or use them on the vine for more drama.

Arrange the prosciutto on the bottom halves of the buns and place the burrata and grapes on top. Drizzle with a little olive oil, sprinkle with basil and pepper, and (try to) place a top on each bun—or enjoy as open sandwiches.

Melted Taleggio Sandwich with Mushrooms and Apple

MAKES 1 SANDWICH

2 teaspoons unsalted butter

½ medium apple, cored and cut into slices

Fine sea salt

Finely ground pepper

3 medium king oyster mushrooms, cut in half lengthwise

1 rustic white bun, cut in half

1 ounce (30 g) Taleggio (or any sweet cheese), cut into thick slices

In this hearty sandwich, Taleggio slowly melts over pan-seared king oyster mushrooms and apple slices, wrapping them in fruity sweetness. It's the kind of comfort food that instantly makes you feel good and that a melted cheese sandwich delivers so reliably. There aren't many treats that help a sobbing heart, mellow swinging moods, or simply sober you up with such ease. You could slip in a slice or two of crispy bacon—that's definitely not a bad idea—but the meatless version is just as stunning. Taleggio is great for any cheese and fruit sandwiches, but fontina, Robiola, or the heartier Comté would also do a good job here.

Set the oven to broil (quicker method) or preheat to 500°F (260°C).*

In a medium, heavy pan, heat 1 teaspoon of the butter over medium-high heat. Add the apple slices and sear, flipping once, for about 2 minutes or until golden brown. Season with a little salt and pepper and transfer to a plate, but leave the pan on the heat.

Add the remaining 1 teaspoon of butter to the pan over medium-high heat. Add the king oyster mushrooms and sear for about 1 minute per side or until golden and al dente. Remove the pan from the heat and season the mushrooms to taste with salt and pepper.

Place the apple slices on the bottom half of the bun and layer the mushrooms and Taleggio on top of the apple. Put the sandwich under the broiler, or roast at 500°F (260°C), for a few minutes or until the cheese starts to melt. Sprinkle with a little pepper and place the top on the bun. Squeeze and enjoy!

* If you don't want to turn on the oven to melt the cheese, you can place the assembled open sandwich in a pan, covered with a lid, over medium-high heat for a couple of minutes or until the cheese starts to melt; mind that the bottom of the bun doesn't burn. Place the top on the bun afterward.

Seared Fig and Chèvre Tartine

MAKES 4 SMALL TARTINES

4 large fresh figs, cut in half

1 tablespoon honey

3 ounces (85 g) aged chèvre log, cut into 8 slices

4 slices baguette

1 teaspoon fresh thyme leaves

You don't really need a recipe for this but maybe a reminder: Fresh figs, baguette, chèvre, and a drizzle of honey—perhaps a glass of fizzy cider or rosé, too—is all you need for a summer picnic, which I encourage you to enjoy midweek. If you still have some work waiting for you after lunch, skip the booze, but indulge in these petite tartines that need less than five minutes. The honey-dripping little bites remind me of short trips to Alsace in early September—stopping the car for a spontaneous picnic, sitting on an old bench in the warming sun, and convinced that I could live on cheese and baguette for the rest of my life.

Heat a small, heavy pan over high heat, without adding any fat, until the pan is hot. Add the figs, skin-side down, and sear for 50 seconds, then flip and sear for 10 seconds; mind that the figs still hold their shape. Remove the pan from the heat and transfer the figs to a plate, then add the honey to the hot pan and let it melt.

Divide the chèvre among the slices of baguette and arrange the figs on top. Drizzle with the warm honey, sprinkle with the thyme, and enjoy immediately.

Arugula Obatzda on a Pretzel Bun

MAKES 3 TO 4 SANDWICHES

4 ounces (110 g) mild Camembert

3 ounces (85 g) cream cheese

1 large handful arugula leaves (about 1 ounce / 30 g), plus a few leaves for serving

1 tablespoon heavy cream

3 to 4 pretzel buns (or spelt or rye buns), cut in half

15 to 20 red radishes, cut into quarters

Coarsely ground pepper

Up for a Bavarian Brotzeit (snack)? It's time for good bread and simple but tasty toppings—and obatzda is just the right choice for this endeavor. It's a popular dip, or spread, in Bavaria, made of Camembert and cream cheese. It's great on dark bread but perfect for salty pretzels or pretzel buns. While traditionally it's mixed with caraway seeds and sweet paprika, I like to introduce green flavors, like fresh herbs or arugula. They balance out its rich and creamy side, making it a bit fresher. Top it off with crisp radishes, cucumber, or cherry tomatoes for a proper Brotzeit.

In a food processor or blender, purée the Camembert, cream cheese, arugula, and heavy cream until smooth; transfer to a bowl.

Spread the obatzda on the bottom halves of the buns and arrange the radishes and a few arugula leaves on top. Sprinkle with a little pepper and place a top on each bun. Enjoy immediately, or, for a picnic, pack the obatzda, radishes, and buns separately and assemble just before serving.

Strawberry and Roquefort Tartine with Hot Salami

MAKES 3 SMALL TARTINES

9 very thin slices hot salami, such as spianata piccante calabrese or Spanish chorizo

3 slices baguette or ciabatta

1 ounce (30 g) Roquefort or Stilton, crumbled

6 medium strawberries, cut in half lengthwise

Coarsely ground pepper

For this tartine, you want to go for really hot salami. Crumbly, mature blue cheese that is sharp and tangy, as well as sweet and ripe strawberries, can handle fiery heat. Ideally, the salami is thinly sliced and delicate, like spianata piccante from Calabria, but Spanish chorizo salami works as well—it's just a bit rougher. When it comes to choosing the right cheese, British Stilton would certainly do a good job, but French Roquefort, made of sheep's milk, pushes it a little further to the edge, which is good. You can enjoy this open sandwich all year round, but only the ripest strawberries, picked at the peak of their season, will be able to properly play with such powerful companions.

Divide the salami among the baguette slices. Arrange the Roquefort and strawberries on top and sprinkle with a little pepper. It won't harm or improve them if you let them sit for an hour or so. Enjoy!

Grilled Gruyère Sandwich
with Pear and Rosemary Ham

MAKES 2 SANDWICHES

2 rustic white buns, cut in half

4 large, very thin slices rosemary ham (or regular ham)

1 medium pear, cored and cut into thin wedges

2 ounces (60 g) Gruyère or Comté, cut into thick slices

About 1 teaspoon roughly chopped fresh rosemary

Coarsely ground pepper

Aromatic Gruyère or Comté, melting and crackling under the broiler, smells and tastes strong, hearty, and a little smoky. It happily mingles with any fruit that's in season: berries, stone fruit, or grapes in the warmer months, or pear to herald autumn and say goodbye to summer. Snuggled with the thinnest slices of Italian rosemary ham, this sandwich makes it easier to look forward to the colder months ahead, and to recipes that are as comforting as chilling on the sofa.

Set the oven to broil (quicker method) or preheat to 500°F (260°C).

Place the bottom halves of the buns in a medium baking dish. Divide the ham between the buns, place the pear wedges on top, and arrange the Gruyère on top of the pear. Place the sandwiches under the broiler, or roast at 500°F (260°C), for a few minutes or until the cheese starts to melt. Sprinkle with a little rosemary and pepper, then place a top on each bun, squeeze a little, and enjoy while the cheese is hot.

5

PASTA

Ricotta and Lemon Spaghetti with Spinach

SERVES 1

3 ounces (85 g) baby spinach
(or trimmed, chopped regular
spinach)

Olive oil, for drizzling

2 to 3 ounces (60 to 85 g)
dried spaghetti

2 to 3 tablespoons fresh
ricotta

½ to 1 tablespoon freshly
grated lemon zest

2 to 3 tablespoons finely
grated Parmesan

Flaky sea salt

Coarsely ground pepper

Spaghetti with ricotta and lemon zest is a dish I can eat for lunch, for dinner, or as a midnight snack. Or for breakfast even, after a long night out. It celebrates such an incredibly simple yet genius combination. For me, ricotta and lemon will always be the taste of the Mediterranean and its way of cooking, capturing the beauty in rural, everyday dishes. There's no need to fuss with this duo, but folding in blanched spinach tastes fantastic and rewards you with the satisfying feeling that you've had your daily veggies.

Bring a medium pot of salted water to a boil and blanch the baby spinach for 1 minute or until tender (if you use regular spinach, blanch it for about 1½ minutes). Transfer to a colander, drain, and quickly rinse with cold water. Leave the spinach in the colander to cool for 2 minutes, then squeeze it a bit, return to the pot, and drizzle with a little olive oil.

Bring a second medium pot of salted water to a boil and cook the spaghetti, according to the package instructions, until al dente. Drain the spaghetti, transfer to a large, deep plate, and drizzle with a little olive oil. Fold the spinach and ricotta into the spaghetti and sprinkle with the lemon zest and Parmesan. Season to taste with salt and pepper and enjoy warm.

Spaghetti with Sun-Dried Tomato Pesto and Burrata

SERVES 2

FOR THE PESTO

2 ounces (60 g) sun-dried tomatoes

1 ounce (30 g) unsalted cashews

¼ cup (60 ml) olive oil

1 handful fresh basil leaves, plus a few small leaves for the topping

FOR THE PASTA

5 to 6 ounces (140 to 170 g) dried spaghetti

1 tablespoon olive oil

4 ounces (110 g) burrata (or mozzarella di bufala), torn in half

Coarsely ground pepper

Sun-dried tomato pesto is another genius pantry gem. Blend the shriveled tomatoes, olive oil, nuts, and some fresh herbs, and you're done. Sometimes I use salted pistachios, but currently, I'm hooked on cashews, which give the pesto a creamy, nutty backbone. Fresh basil lightens it up—parsley would also be fine—but the real game changer in this recipe is a piece of burrata sitting on top of the steaming spaghetti like a queen on her throne. The red pesto is also a wonderful dip for mixed raw vegetables and a scrumptious spread on dark or white crusty bread. You can easily keep the pesto in the fridge for days, so don't hesitate—just double the recipe.

For the pesto, if using jarred sun-dried tomatoes in oil, just drain them, without cooking them, and transfer straight to the food processor. If using sun-dried tomatoes preserved in salt, bring a small pot of water to a boil and cook the tomatoes for about 3 minutes or until soft. Reserve the cooking water, then transfer the tomatoes to a colander, briefly rinse with cold water, and drain for a few minutes.

In a food processor or blender, purée the sun-dried tomatoes, cashews, olive oil, basil, and 4 tablespoons of the reserved cooking water until smooth; add more of the cooking water if the pesto is too dry. If using jarred sun-dried tomatoes in olive oil, you won't have any reserved water and might have to add a little more olive oil. Transfer the pesto to a small bowl and set aside.

For the pasta, bring a large pot of salted water to a boil and cook the spaghetti, according to the package instructions, until al dente. Drain the pasta and return to the pot, then toss with the olive oil. Divide the spaghetti between two plates and place half the burrata in the middle of each plate. Sprinkle with pesto, a little pepper, and the small basil leaves and enjoy!

Mac and Fava Bean Carbonara

SERVES 3 TO 4

11 ounces (310 g) fresh or frozen shelled fava beans (or peas)

3 very fresh large eggs, at room temperature

3 very fresh large egg yolks, at room temperature

Fine sea salt

Coarsely ground pepper

3 ounces (85 g) pecorino or Parmesan, finely grated

11 ounces (310 g) dried macaroni (or any short pasta)

Olive oil, for cooking

3 ounces (85 g) bacon slices, cut into thin strips

My granny Lisa used to make carbonara with macaroni pasta and not spaghetti. I still remember the smell of the bacon sizzling in her kitchen. Figuring out the right formula for the egg mixture is the tricky part of carbonara, but I find using an equal amount of whole eggs and egg yolks leads to the most satisfying result. The macaroni comes out silky, evenly coated with eggs, and wonderfully creamy. Carbonara shouldn't be dry, yet the pasta shouldn't swim in egg either. Blanched fava beans make it feel lighter, or you could also use fresh or frozen peas. No offense to carbs and eggs, but a little green definitely enhances the carbonara experience.

Bring a medium pot of salted water to a boil and blanch the fava beans for 5 minutes or until tender (if you use peas, blanch them for 1 minute). Transfer to a colander, drain, and briefly rinse with cold water, then set aside.

In a large bowl, whisk together the eggs, egg yolks, a little salt, and a generous amount of pepper. Whisk in two-thirds of the pecorino and set the bowl aside.

Bring a large pot of salted water to a boil and cook the macaroni, according to the package instructions, until al dente.

While the pasta is boiling, cook the bacon: In a medium, heavy pan, heat a small splash of olive oil over medium-high heat and cook the bacon, stirring occasionally, for 5 minutes or until crispy; set the pan aside.

When the pasta is done, drain briefly and immediately transfer to the bowl with the egg-pecorino mixture. Add the bacon and the bacon fat from the pan, then add the fava beans and gently but quickly toss to combine. Season to taste with salt and pepper. Divide the pasta among plates, sprinkle with the remaining pecorino and a little pepper, and serve immediately.

Spaghetti with Sausage Meatballs and Tomato Sauce

SERVES 1

1 large Italian sausage, or any coarse sausage, skin removed and cut into small pieces

Olive oil, for cooking

1 large clove garlic

1 teaspoon fennel seeds, crushed with a mortar and pestle, plus ¼ teaspoon whole seeds for serving

1 small bay leaf

1 tablespoon tomato paste

1 teaspoon balsamic vinegar

14 ounces (400 g) canned whole peeled tomatoes, chopped

Fine sea salt

Finely ground pepper

2 to 3 ounces (60 to 85 g) dried spaghetti

A few fresh basil leaves, for serving

Let's say you feel like polpette al sugo—tiny meatballs stuffed with herbs and spices in a rich tomato sauce—but you're not in the mood to make meatballs from scratch. There's no need to give way to despair. Here's a lazy ten-minute version! Take a large Italian sausage, or any coarse well-seasoned sausage, and remove the skin, then cut it into small pieces and roll into tiny meatballs. Done. All you have to do is brown them in a hot pan for a few minutes, then finish cooking them in a sweet tomato sauce, refined with bay leaf and fennel seeds. Toss your quick ragù with steaming spaghetti and it will feel like sitting on a Tuscan piazza.

Wet your hands a little and roll the sausage pieces into tiny meatballs.

In a large, heavy pan, heat a splash of olive oil over medium-high heat. Add the meatballs and cook, turning occasionally, for 5 minutes; reduce the heat to medium if they brown too quickly. Add the whole garlic, fennel seeds, and bay leaf and cook, stirring, for 20 seconds. Add the tomato paste and vinegar, stir, and cook for 10 seconds, then add the tomatoes and season with salt and pepper. Cook over medium-high heat, stirring occasionally, for about 7 minutes or until the sauce is thick. Season to taste with salt and pepper.

While the sauce is cooking, bring a medium pot of salted water to a boil, then cook the spaghetti, according to the package instructions, until al dente.

Drain, then transfer the spaghetti to a deep plate and arrange the sauce and meatballs on top. Sprinkle with fennel seeds, the basil, and a little pepper and enjoy your lazy version of polpette al sugo.

Fusilli with Pea-Ramp Pesto

SERVES 2

FOR THE PASTA

6 ounces (170 g) dried fusilli
(or any short pasta)

Coarsely ground pepper

FOR THE PESTO

7 ounces (200 g) fresh or
frozen peas

1 ounce (30 g) ramp leaves,
plus 3 sliced ramp leaves
for serving

1 ounce (30 g) Parmesan, plus
2 tablespoons finely grated
Parmesan for serving

3 tablespoons olive oil

2 teaspoons freshly
squeezed lemon juice

Fine sea salt

I love ramp pesto and I love pea pesto, but I only recently combined the two. It creates a gorgeous, thick green pesto that slides into fusilli's spirals, spreading its sweet and garlicky aroma. It's energizing like a sunny day in April. You can enjoy this pasta warm, or even topped with a whole burrata if you're in the mood for a richer treat, but it's also very nice as a cold pasta salad. So, don't worry if you fill your lunch box with this bright green fusilli in the morning and let it sit for a few hours; it won't harm your pleasure in the least bit.

For the pasta, bring a large pot of salted water to a boil and cook the fusilli, according to the package instructions, until al dente.

Meanwhile, for the pesto, bring a small pot of salted water to a boil and blanch the peas for 1 minute. Reserve ¼ cup (60 ml) of the cooking water and set aside. Transfer the peas to a colander, drain, and briefly rinse with cold water. Measure 2 ounces (60 g) of the peas and set aside. Transfer the remaining peas to a food processor or blender, add 3 tablespoons of the reserved cooking water, ramp leaves, Parmesan, olive oil, and lemon juice, and purée until smooth. Add more of the cooking water if the pesto is too dry and season to taste with salt.

When the pasta is done, drain the fusilli, and divide between two plates. Fold in the pesto and the reserved peas, then sprinkle with the sliced ramp leaves and grated Parmesan. Season with a little pepper and enjoy warm or cold.

Gnocchetti Sardi with Butter Bean–Basil Pesto and Tomatoes

SERVES 2

FOR THE PESTO

1¼ cups (250 g) drained and rinsed canned butter beans (lima beans; or cannellini beans)

2 tablespoons olive oil

1 handful fresh basil leaves, plus a few small leaves for serving

Fine sea salt

Coarsely ground pepper

FOR THE PASTA

6 ounces (170 g) dried gnocchetti sardi (or any short pasta)

1 tablespoon olive oil

8 cherry or grape tomatoes, cut in half lengthwise

Because they're so versatile, tasty, and convenient, canned legumes are one of my favorite pantry staples—you can always rely on them. Butter beans or cannellini beans are an especially fabulous foundation for a quick and nourishing puréed pesto. Add whatever fresh herbs you can find on your windowsill (basil is particularly nice) and pour in a little olive oil for a pesto that feels light but won't leave you hungry. You can mix it with gnocchetti sardi, or any other short pasta, and fold in tiny tomatoes, shifting the focus from carbs to vegetables. Easy to prepare in advance, this pesto is also a great addition to sandwiches. Imagine layering it with roasted eggplant and bacon in a crusty bun the next day (page 157). So good.

For the pesto, purée the butter beans, olive oil, and basil in a food processor or blender until smooth. Season to taste with salt and pepper.

For the pasta, bring a large pot of salted water to a boil and cook the gnocchetti sardi, according to the package instructions, until al dente. Drain the pasta and return to the pot, then toss with the olive oil.

Divide the pasta between two bowls, top with the pesto and tomatoes, and season to taste with salt and pepper. Sprinkle with small basil leaves and enjoy warm or cold.

Ciceri e tria—Chickpeas and Pasta with Mushrooms

SERVES 2

4 to 5 ounces (110 to 140 g) dried spaghetti

Olive oil, for searing

2 teaspoons unsalted butter

5 ounces (140 g) medium king oyster mushrooms, cut in half lengthwise

Fine sea salt

Finely ground pepper

1¼ cups (250 g) drained and rinsed canned chickpeas

⅓ cup (75 ml) freshly squeezed orange juice, plus more to taste

2 tablespoons finely grated Parmesan

1 small handful fresh basil leaves

Ciceri e tria translates to "chickpeas and pasta" and is a popular dish in Puglia, at the heel of Italy's boot. Traditionally, it's made with chickpeas and the ribbon-shaped pasta known as tria, and crowned with fried pasta. To keep it light and simple, I leave out the fried carbs and use canned legumes rather than dried. It's much quicker to prepare and we can use the saved time to be a bit playful. I added sautéed zucchini and orange zest to a ciceri e tria recipe in my first book, *eat in my kitchen*, but here, we think more of autumn. Briefly cooked king oyster mushrooms, firm and juicy, are folded into warm spaghetti, bringing in an earthy character. If you can find them, chanterelles would also be a good choice.

Bring a large pot of salted water to a boil and cook the spaghetti, according to the package instructions, until al dente. Reserve ¼ cup (60 ml) of the cooking water and set aside, then drain the spaghetti, return to the pot, and cover.

Meanwhile, in a medium, heavy pan, heat a splash of olive oil and the butter over medium–high heat. Add the king oyster mushrooms and sear for about 1 minute per side or until golden brown and al dente. Remove the pan from the heat, season the mushrooms to taste with salt and pepper, and transfer to a plate.

Return the pan to medium–high heat, add a little olive oil and the chickpeas, and cook for 1 minute. Season with a little salt and pepper, then add the orange juice and 3 tablespoons of the reserved cooking water. Gently fold in the spaghetti and mushrooms, then season to taste with salt, pepper, and additional orange juice. Add more of the cooking water if the pasta is too dry.

Divide the spaghetti, chickpeas, and mushrooms between two plates, sprinkle with the Parmesan and basil, and enjoy.

Spaghetti with Pesto Meatballs and Seared Tomatoes

SERVES 2 TO 3

FOR THE PESTO

1 ounce (30 g) fresh basil leaves, plus a few small leaves for serving

3 tablespoons finely grated Parmesan, plus 2 tablespoons for serving

1 tablespoon cashews or pine nuts

¼ cup (60 ml) olive oil

Fine sea salt

FOR THE MEATBALLS

9 ounces (250 g) ground beef

3 tablespoons dry breadcrumbs

½ beaten large egg

1 small shallot, finely chopped

1½ tablespoons pesto

1½ teaspoons olive oil, plus more for cooking

¾ teaspoon fine sea salt

Finely ground pepper

1½ tablespoons unsalted butter

FOR THE PASTA

5 to 6 ounces (140 to 170 g) dried spaghetti

12 cherry or grape tomatoes

Adding basil pesto to the mixture for little meatballs makes them juicier and tastier. And if you use the fat the meatballs cooked in to sear whole cherry or grape tomatoes and then toss in warm spaghetti, you'll end up with a pasta that's perfectly balanced between hearty and summery. You can use store-bought pesto, but it will never taste as good as a vibrant green pesto lovingly made with your own hands.

For the pesto, purée the basil, Parmesan, cashews, and olive oil in a food processor or blender until smooth, then season to taste with salt.

For the meatballs, combine the ground beef, bread-crumbs, egg, shallot, 1½ tablespoons of pesto, the 1½ teaspoons of olive oil, salt, and a generous amount of pepper in a medium bowl and mix with your hands until well combined. Form the mixture into 12 small meatballs and transfer to a large plate.

In a large, heavy pan, heat a generous splash of olive oil and the butter over medium-high heat. Add the meat-balls and cook, turning occasionally and reducing the heat, if necessary, for 8 minutes or until golden brown and cooked through.

Meanwhile, for the pasta, bring a large pot of salted water to a boil and cook the spaghetti, according to the package instructions, until al dente. Drain the spaghetti, return to the pot, and cover.

cont'd

When the meatballs are done, transfer them to a large plate and pour all but about 1 tablespoon of the fat from the pan into a heat-resistant bowl and set aside. Place the pan with the fat over medium-high heat, add the tomatoes, and cook, shaking the pan occasionally, for about 3 minutes or until the tomatoes are golden brown and still holding their shape but starting to soften. Gently fold in the spaghetti and meatballs, adding some of the reserved fat if the pasta is too dry, and season to taste with salt and pepper.

Divide the pasta among large, deep plates, drizzle with the remaining pesto, and sprinkle with Parmesan and basil leaves. Enjoy warm.

Green Vegetable Pasta with Bozen Sauce

SERVES 2

FOR THE BOZEN SAUCE

2 tablespoons olive oil

1 tablespoon freshly squeezed lemon juice

1 teaspoon Dijon mustard

2 hard-boiled large eggs, cut into tiny cubes

Fine sea salt

Finely ground pepper

FOR THE PASTA

5 ounces (140 g) dried farfalle (bow tie pasta)

4 ounces (110 g) trimmed Romano beans (or other green beans)

5 ounces (140 g) trimmed green asparagus

3 ounces (85 g) fresh or frozen peas

1 tablespoon olive oil

Fine sea salt

Finely ground pepper

2 tablespoons chopped chives

A plate full of bow tie–shaped pasta, dotted with green vegetables and a chunky sauce made of chopped hard-boiled eggs, mustard, and olive oil, is more than a scrumptious stunner. It's a breath of fresh spring air swiping roots and cabbages off the daily menu—and the kitchen counter. In spring, after many months of limited supply from the vegetable kingdom, the palate will be relieved: Winter's finally over! This sauce originated in the capital city of South Tyrol, Bolzano, in northern Italy. Usually served with white or green asparagus and potatoes, it works just as well with pasta and makes the farfalle rich and silky. Like most of the recipes in this chapter, you can enjoy this dish warm or cold. Just toss it all together, pack it in a lunch box, and eat it outside, sitting on a bench in the first warming rays of spring.

For the Bozen sauce, whisk together the olive oil, lemon juice, and mustard in a medium bowl, stir in the eggs, and season to taste with salt and pepper.

For the pasta, bring a large pot of salted water to a boil and cook the pasta, according to the package instructions, until al dente.

Meanwhile, bring a second large pot of salted water to a boil and blanch the beans for about 5 minutes or until tender. Leave the pot on the heat and, using a slotted ladle, transfer the beans to a colander. Briefly rinse with cold water, then cut into bite-size pieces and set aside. Add the asparagus to the boiling water and blanch for about 3 minutes or until al dente, then add the peas to the asparagus and cook for 1 minute. Drain the asparagus and peas, briefly rinse with cold water, and cut the asparagus into bite-size pieces.

cont'd

When the farfalle is done, drain and return to the pot. Stir in the olive oil, then fold in the beans, asparagus, and peas and season with a little salt and pepper; mind that the sauce is also seasoned. Divide the farfalle and vegetables between two plates, drizzle with the Bozen sauce, and sprinkle with the chives. You can enjoy this pasta warm or as a cold salad, adding the Bozen sauce just before serving.

Pasta Salad with Belgian Endive, Fennel, and Bell Pepper

6 ounces (170 g) dried fusilli or farfalle pasta

¼ cup (60 ml) olive oil, plus more to taste

3 tablespoons freshly squeezed lemon juice, plus more to taste

Fine sea salt

Finely ground pepper

½ medium fennel bulb, cored and thinly sliced lengthwise, plus a few chopped fennel fronds

½ medium yellow bell pepper, cut into cubes

12 red or yellow Belgian endive leaves, thickly sliced

Coarsely ground pepper

Pasta dishes usually don't need many ingredients to shine. Keeping the recipe pure and simple is often best, but a summery pasta salad can also be lavish. You want a bold play of colors, textures, and flavors, joyfully bouncing on your tongue. Bitter red Belgian endive, sweet bell pepper, and crisp fennel keep the palate—and the eyes—well entertained. Mingling with twisted fusilli and a fresh lemon-olive oil dressing, this is a light dish, ideal for a quick lunch or weekend BBQ with friends.

Bring a large pot of salted water to a boil and cook the pasta, according to the package instructions, until al dente. Drain and transfer to a large bowl or deep platter.

Whisk together the olive oil and lemon juice in a small bowl, then season with a little salt and finely ground pepper. Add to the pasta, toss to coat, and season to taste with salt and pepper.

Fold the fennel bulb, bell pepper, and Belgian endive into the pasta, adding more olive oil and lemon juice to taste. Sprinkle with a little coarsely ground pepper and the fennel fronds. Enjoy warm or cold.

Mac and Ricotta with Lemon and Peas

SERVES 2

7 ounces (200 g) dried macaroni (or any short pasta)

4 ounces (110 g) fresh or frozen peas (or fava beans)

4 ounces (110 g) fresh ricotta

1 tablespoon freshly grated lemon zest

¼ cup (60 ml) freshly squeezed lemon juice

1 ounce (30 g) finely grated Parmesan, plus 1 tablespoon for the topping

Fine sea salt

Coarsely ground pepper

Mac and cheese has always fascinated me. It's the essence of comfort food, a beloved childhood memory of many of my American friends, and it's a super quick lunch. However, even after eating a small portion of it, I need a nap. The roux of flour and butter combined with Cheddar is heavy, so to lighten it up, I replace all that with only fresh ricotta and a little Parmesan. Blanched peas, fresh or frozen, help balance the carbs without stealing the spotlight. If you find fava beans at the market, you can also use them. Lots of lemon zest and juice politely push this dish in a more citrusy direction and turn it into a summer version of mac and cheese.

Bring a large pot of salted water to a boil and cook the macaroni, according to the package instructions, until al dente.

Meanwhile, bring a small pot of salted water to a boil and blanch the peas for 1 minute (if you use fava beans, blanch them for 5 minutes). Transfer to a colander, drain, and briefly rinse with cold water, then set aside.

Reserve ⅓ cup (75 ml) of the cooking water, then drain the macaroni and return to the pot. Add the ricotta, lemon zest, lemon juice, Parmesan, and half of the reserved cooking water and stir until well combined and smooth. Add more of the pasta water if the pasta is too dry. Stir in the peas and season to taste with salt and pepper.

Divide the pasta between two bowls, sprinkle with a little Parmesan and pepper, and enjoy warm.

Spaghetti with Rainbow Chard and Preserved Lemon

SERVES 2

11 ounces (310 g) trimmed rainbow or regular chard

5 to 6 ounces (140 to 170 g) dried spaghetti

Olive oil, for cooking

2 tablespoons very thinly sliced preserved lemon

½ cup (120 ml) freshly squeezed tangerine or orange juice

Fine sea salt

Finely ground pepper

1 to 2 teaspoons freshly grated lemon zest (optional)

You won't find many condiments, pickles, and preserves in my fridge, but there's always a jar of preserved lemons stuck between the mustard, olives, and anchovies. As much as I like to preserve them myself, sometimes I'm just lazy and get them from the store. Instantly bringing in a piquant touch, they are a very convenient way to boost pasta, roasted vegetables, meat, and sandwiches. If all of this sounds too fussy, you can also use freshly squeezed lemon juice. You'll miss out on the sharp, biting note that comes with the preserved citrus, but if you're generous with the juice, it will still work.

Slice the chard stalks very thinly. Cut the chard leaves in half lengthwise, then cut them into finger-thick slices.

Bring a large pot of salted water to a boil and cook the spaghetti, according to the package instructions, until al dente. Drain the spaghetti, return to the pot, and cover.

Meanwhile, in a large, heavy pan, heat a generous splash of olive oil over medium-high heat. Add the preserved lemon and cook, stirring constantly, for 45 seconds. Reduce the heat to medium, then add the chard stalks and sauté, stirring occasionally, for 8 minutes or until al dente. Add the chard leaves and a little olive oil, turn the heat up to medium-high, and sauté, stirring occasionally, for 3 minutes. Deglaze the pan with the tangerine juice, stir, and season with a little salt and pepper. Cook for 1 minute, then take the pan off the heat. Fold the spaghetti into the chard and season to taste with salt and pepper. Divide the spaghetti between two plates, sprinkle with a little lemon zest, and serve warm.

Broccoli Pesto Pasta

SERVES 2

8 ounces (225 g) broccoli florets

2 ounces (60 g) unsalted cashews, plus a few chopped cashews for the topping

¼ cup (60 ml) olive oil

2 teaspoons freshly grated lemon zest, plus more for the topping

4 teaspoons freshly squeezed lemon juice

Fine sea salt

Finely ground pepper

5 to 6 ounces (140 to 170 g) dried casarecce pasta (or any short pasta)

Coarsely ground pepper

Broccoli and I have a bit of a difficult relationship. The vegetable needs to work quite hard to earn a place in my kitchen. Usually, I solve this by pairing it with very bold—you might even call them overpowering—ingredients. However, in this recipe, I'm taking a different approach. Broccoli-cashew pesto emphasizes the cabbage's sweet side, while lemon zest and juice give it a tangy freshness. This pesto makes me feel like I'm eating lunch in Palermo, so I go for Sicilian casarecce pasta. Short and twisty, casarecce is perfect for collecting the green pesto, but any similar pasta shape is fine. You could even use spaghetti, but seeing that leftovers make a really nice cold pasta salad, I prefer shorter shapes.

Bring a medium pot of salted water to a boil and blanch the broccoli for about 3 minutes or until tender. Reserve about 1 cup (240 ml) of the cooking water, then drain the broccoli and briefly rinse with cold water. Set 6 small florets aside for the topping.

In a food processor or blender, purée the remaining broccoli, ⅔ cup (150 ml) of the reserved cooking water, the cashews, olive oil, lemon zest, and lemon juice until smooth. Add more of the cooking water if the pesto is too dry. Season to taste with salt and finely ground pepper.

Bring a large pot of salted water to a boil and cook the pasta, according to the package instructions, until al dente. Drain the pasta and return to the pot.

You can either mix the warm pasta and the pesto in a large bowl or divide the pasta between individual bowls and add dollops of pesto. Sprinkle with chopped cashews, a little lemon zest, and coarsely ground pepper and top with the reserved broccoli florets. Enjoy warm or cold.

Farfalle with Artichoke-Ricotta Pesto, Tomatoes, and Olives

SERVES 2

FOR THE PESTO

5 ounces (140 g) artichoke hearts, marinated in olive oil, drained, plus 1 large artichoke heart, cut into 6 wedges, for serving

3 ounces (85 g) fresh ricotta

1 tablespoon olive oil

2 teaspoons freshly squeezed lemon juice

Fine sea salt

Finely ground pepper

FOR THE PASTA

5 to 6 ounces (140 to 170 g) dried farfalle pasta (or any short pasta)

1 tablespoon olive oil, plus more as needed

6 cherry or grape tomatoes, sliced

6 large Kalamata olives, pitted and sliced

Fine sea salt

Finely ground pepper

When you purée marinated artichoke hearts and ricotta and use it as a pesto with farfalle, you might be surprised. It's velvety and chunky, and pleasantly balances sweet and sour notes. Folding in fresh tomatoes and dark Kalamata olives instantly gives the pasta a breezy vibe. The fruity, briny, and bitter tones lend the smooth composition more depth, but it comes easy. You could also add chopped fresh basil or parsley, or chives even, especially if you see this recipe more like a pasta salad.

For the pesto, purée the 5 ounces (140 g) of artichoke hearts, ricotta, olive oil, and lemon juice in a food processor or blender until smooth and season to taste with salt and pepper; set the pesto aside.

For the pasta, bring a large pot of salted water to a boil and cook the farfalle, according to the package instructions, until al dente.

Meanwhile, heat a splash of olive oil in a small, heavy pan over medium-high heat. Add the artichoke heart wedges and sear for 1 minute on each cut side. Take the pan off the heat.

Drain the farfalle, return to the pot, and toss with the 1 tablespoon of olive oil, then divide the pasta, tomatoes, and olives between two plates. Plop generous dollops of the artichoke pesto on top of the farfalle and arrange the seared artichoke wedges on top. Add more olive oil if the pasta is too dry, season to taste with salt and pepper, and enjoy. Alternatively, you can mix everything together in a large bowl and then divide it between two plates. It won't look as pretty and it's also more convenient to adjust the amount of pesto for each serving.

SEAFOOD

Tuna with Tomato-Olive Salsa

SERVES 1

FOR THE SALSA

1 medium, ripe tomato, cut into tiny cubes

6 green olives, pitted and roughly chopped

6 large fresh basil leaves, thinly sliced

1 teaspoon tomato paste

1 teaspoon olive oil

½ teaspoon balsamic vinegar

Fine sea salt

Coarsely ground pepper

FOR THE TUNA

Olive oil, for searing

1 (7-ounce / 200 g) tuna steak, about 1¼ inches (3 cm) thick

Flaky sea salt

Coarsely ground pepper

We tend to think of fish or seafood dishes as too complicated and labor-intensive, even for dinnertime, let alone midday—but they're often quicker to prepare than a salad. Tuna steak is particularly easy to handle. The texture is robust, while the taste is strong, which means you can relax, be brave, and start experimenting. Thanks to a speedy tomato salsa with green olives and fresh basil, this dish is the perfect solution when you're craving a light seafood lunch. I prefer to cook tuna steak in the pan and not in the oven, and just long enough that the fish starts to flake but is still a little pink in the middle. Be careful not to overcook tuna or it will end up being too dry. That wouldn't be a big deal if you use it cold in a salad, but here you want it to be tender and juicy when you drizzle it with the sweet and sour red salsa.

For the salsa, mix together the tomato, olives, basil, tomato paste, olive oil, and vinegar in a medium bowl, season to taste with fine sea salt and pepper, and set aside.

For the tuna, heat a splash of olive oil in a medium, heavy pan over high heat. Add the tuna, reduce the heat to medium-high, and cook for 3 minutes. Flip the tuna and cook for 3 minutes or until flaky but still pink inside; reduce the heat if it browns too quickly. If you prefer tuna completely done and cooked through, cook it for another minute on each side over medium heat. Season to taste with flaky sea salt and pepper and transfer to a plate. Arrange some of the salsa around and on top of the tuna and enjoy while the tuna is hot.

Keep leftover tuna and salsa, covered, in the fridge to use in a salad the next day, adding some torn green lettuce leaves.

Salmon Ceviche with Dill and Juniper Berries

SERVES 1

1 teaspoon flaky sea salt

2 large juniper berries

2 tablespoons freshly squeezed lemon juice

2 tablespoons freshly squeezed lime juice

1½ tablespoons roughly chopped fresh dill, plus 1 teaspoon for serving

1 (6-ounce / 170 g) sushi-quality, skinless salmon fillet, cut into ¼-inch-thick (0.5 cm) slices crosswise

½ teaspoon freshly grated lemon zest, for serving

My mother and all her siblings make fabulous gravlax, curing a whole salmon in a salt-sugar mixture with lots of dill and juniper berries. It's one of the treats that gets the most attention at our food-focused family gatherings. I liked the idea of picking up on their recipe and turning it into a quick salmon ceviche, letting the raw fish cure in lime and lemon juice for just a few minutes. Juniper berries' pungent taste reminds me of pine and citrus. To make sure that it gets the attention it deserves, I grind the dark berries with sea salt and use it to season the ceviche. In combination with lemon zest and fresh dill, it gets along very harmoniously with the tender salmon. If you don't have juniper berries, which are usually easy to find in the spice section of supermarkets, you could leave them out. The recipe will still work, but you'll miss out on the flavor that is so typical of gravlax.

Using a mortar and pestle, pound and grind the salt and juniper berries until fine, then set aside.

In a large deep plate, whisk together the lemon juice, lime juice, and the 1½ tablespoons of dill. Add the salmon, gently toss to coat, and marinate for 3 minutes. Remove the salmon from the citrus mixture, discarding the mixture, and arrange the salmon on a large plate. Season to taste with the juniper salt and sprinkle with the remaining 1 teaspoon of dill and the lemon zest. Enjoy immediately.

Lime Mussels with Zucchini and Cilantro

SERVES 2 TO 3

2¼ pounds (1 kg) fresh mussels

8 ounces (225 g) zucchini, cut into tiny cubes

1 cup (240 ml) dry white wine

1 tablespoon freshly grated lime zest, plus ½ tablespoon for serving

⅓ cup (75 ml) freshly squeezed lime juice

¼ cup (60 ml) freshly squeezed orange juice

1 small bunch fresh marjoram

1 small bunch fresh cilantro, plus 1 large handful cilantro leaves for serving

2 medium bay leaves

1 teaspoon fine sea salt

1 baguette, for serving (optional)

This recipe is fresh and easy like a morning swim in the sea. Zucchini, lime, and cilantro confidently complement tender mussels, which cook for just five minutes. Buy them pre-rinsed and ready-to-eat and you'll only need to rinse them briefly under cold water just before cooking them. This dish is practically made for a Saturday lunch with friends but is still manageable for a quick weekday treat just for you. Serve it with crunchy baguette and a glass of crisp white wine and it will feel like sitting at a French seaside restaurant. You can use any leftover cooked mussels for a quick fish soup (page 126), but remove them from their shells and keep them covered in the fridge for no more than a day.

Rinse the mussels briefly with cold water and pull off their beards. Discard any broken mussels.

In a large pot, combine the zucchini, white wine, the 1 tablespoon of lime zest, lime juice, orange juice, bunches of marjoram and cilantro, bay leaves, and salt and bring to a boil. Add the mussels, reduce the heat to medium, cover, and cook for 5 minutes or until the shells open. Shake the pot once or twice while the mussels are cooking or gently stir them with a slotted ladle or spoon. Discard the bunches of marjoram and cilantro and any mussels that don't open. Add the remaining ½ tablespoon of lime zest and the cilantro leaves, stir, and immediately divide the mussels, zucchini, and broth among bowls. Serve with the fresh baguette.

Salmon with Coriander Crust and Lemon Butter

SERVES 1

1 tablespoon coriander seeds, lightly crushed with a mortar and pestle

1 large egg white

1 (9-ounce / 250 g) skin-on salmon fillet

Olive oil, for cooking

Fine sea salt

1 tablespoon unsalted butter

1 tablespoon freshly squeezed lemon juice

Covering a fillet with a crunchy spice crust and cooking it in a hot pan is my favorite way of preparing salmon. It's an oily fish, so it needs the heat to burn off some of its fat. The fact that it's so rich isn't bad, as it keeps the fillet juicy, but it does benefit from losing some of the fat. For the crust, you can go for peppercorns packed with heat, sweet fennel seeds, or coriander seeds, which lend the salmon a citrusy note. Serving the fillet with a quick sizzling lemon butter highlights the citrusy quality of the coriander.

Spread the coriander seeds on a flat plate, giving them the shape of the salmon fillet. Add the egg white to a deep plate and whisk briefly. Dip just the skinless side of the salmon in the egg wash and then in the coriander seeds, gently pressing the salmon fillet into the coriander seeds.

In a medium, heavy pan, heat a splash of olive oil over medium-high heat. Add the salmon, skin-side down, and cook for 7 minutes. Reduce the heat to medium-low and gently turn the salmon over; mind that the coriander seeds don't fall off and add a little more oil to the pan if it's too dry. Cook the salmon, depending on its thickness, for another 8 to 11 minutes or until flaky but still pink inside. Season the salmon with a little salt and transfer to a plate.

Add the butter to the pan and melt over medium-high heat until sizzling. Add the lemon juice and whisk for 10 seconds. Drizzle the lemon butter around the salmon fillet and enjoy immediately. Keep left-over salmon, covered, in the fridge to use for pasta or salads the next day.

Béné's Shrimp Cocktail

SERVES 3 TO 4

⅓ cup (75 g) mayonnaise

2 tablespoons ketchup

2 teaspoons cognac

4 to 5 drops Tabasco
(or any hot sauce)

Freshly grated orange
zest, to taste

1 pound (450 g) shelled and
cooked medium shrimp or
prawns, cold

2 large Belgian endives, very
thinly sliced crosswise

2 tangerines (or 1 orange),
peeled (skin and white
pith removed) and cut
into segments

Shrimp cocktail may sound very seventies, a little old-fashioned and dusty. However, I was quickly converted when my friend Bénédict Berna of Berlin's Rhinoçéros Bar placed a cocktail glass filled with the firm seafood bites, covered in a pink dressing, in front of me. Not many dishes manage to balance comfort and excitement, simplicity and extravagance, quite so effortlessly. And, if you use cooked shrimp, you can whip it all up in five minutes. A shrimp cocktail is so much more than an appetizer. A few slices of fresh baguette on the side and it's basically the queen of quick and lazy seafood lunches.

In a large bowl, whisk together the mayonnaise, ketchup, cognac, Tabasco, and a little orange zest. Add the shrimp and toss to combine.

Divide the Belgian endive, shrimp, and tangerine segments among 3 to 4 bowls or wide champagne glasses and serve immediately.

MEAT

Roasted Chicken Breast with Peach–Cilantro–Ginger Salsa

SERVES 1

FOR THE SALSA*

1 large yellow peach

1 large white doughnut peach

1 tablespoon finely chopped fresh cilantro, plus a few chopped leaves for serving

½ to 1 teaspoon finely grated fresh ginger

2 teaspoons freshly squeezed lemon juice

1 teaspoon olive oil

⅛ teaspoon fine sea salt

FOR THE CHICKEN

Olive oil, for searing

1 medium boneless, skinless chicken breast

Flaky sea salt

Coarsely ground pepper

The true star in this recipe is the peach salsa—no offense to the chicken. Briefly seared and finished off in the oven, the meat is perfectly tender, but the salsa has the kind of easy playfulness that creates pure joy in a dish. The result is layers of bold flavor, without drifting into anything complicated. You can substitute the peaches with dark plums—use three plums in place of the two types of peaches—which are easier to find throughout the year and create a more tart salsa than the sweeter peaches. Ginger and fresh cilantro, used generously, give the chicken vibrant pungency.

Preheat the oven to 400°F (200°C).

For the salsa, bring a small pot of water to a boil and blanch both peaches at the same time for 4 to 7 minutes or until you can easily peel off their skin; the cooking time depends on their ripeness. Drain the peaches and, using a knife or your fingers, peel off their skin under running cold water. Transfer the peaches to a cutting board, then cut in half and remove the pits. Chop the peaches roughly and transfer to a medium bowl. Add the cilantro, ½ teaspoon of ginger, lemon juice, olive oil, and fine sea salt and mix gently. Season to taste with additional ginger and set aside.

For the chicken, heat a splash of olive oil in a small, heavy ovenproof skillet over medium-high heat. Add the chicken breast and sear for 1 minute per side. Season with flaky sea salt and pepper, then roast in the oven for about 8 minutes or until the juices run clear when you prick the thickest part of the chicken with a skewer. Transfer the chicken to a plate and let rest for 5 minutes, then drizzle generously with the salsa, sprinkle with the cilantro, and enjoy.

* This is enough salsa for 2 servings. You can either cook 2 chicken breasts or use any remaining salsa for sandwiches or as a condiment with any kind of mature cheese.

Schnitzel with Swabian Potato and Cucumber Salad

SERVES 2

FOR THE SALAD

1 pound (450 g) peeled
waxy potatoes

¼ cup (60 ml) white
balsamic vinegar

¼ cup (60 ml) water

1 medium onion, very
finely diced

4 ounces (110 g) scrubbed
cucumber, cut in half
lengthwise and very
thinly sliced

3 tablespoons olive oil

Fine sea salt

Coarsely ground pepper

FOR THE SCHNITZEL

2 to 3 large, ⅛-inch-thick
(0.3 cm) veal or pork cutlets,
about 11 ounces (310 g) total

½ cup (65 g) all-purpose flour

2 large eggs, beaten

½ cup (70 g) dry breadcrumbs

3 to 4 tablespoons unsalted
butter

Olive oil, for cooking

Fine sea salt

Coarsely ground pepper

My stepfather, Uli, used to love a good schnitzel, but I think he adored the Swabian potato salad that my mother served alongside it even more. He introduced us to this southern German classic, which is easy to make, especially if you have leftover boiled potatoes lying around. There are two ways to prepare it: You can either slice the potatoes or grate them coarsely. Thin cucumber slices and a warm onion vinaigrette keep it light and sweet. If you want to freshen it up, you can fold in small lettuce leaves, such as mesclun, mâche, or arugula. The schnitzel doesn't take long either; just make sure your cutlets are thin and even. Either ask your butcher to do this or flatten them with a meat pounder before you cook them. If you have leftover schnitzel and potato salad, stuff them both in a rustic bun the next day. It's the best German sandwich I can think of.

For the salad, in a medium pot, cover the potatoes with salted water and bring to a boil. Reduce the heat, cover, and simmer for 18 to 20 minutes or until tender. Drain the potatoes, transfer to a plate, and let them cool for a few minutes; you can use them warm or cold.

In a small saucepan, bring the vinegar, water, and onion to a boil. Reduce the heat, cover, and simmer for 3 minutes. Remove the pot from the heat and let it sit, covered, for about 5 minutes.

Grate the potatoes coarsely and transfer to a medium bowl. Add the cucumber, the warm onion–vinegar mixture, and the olive oil, mix gently, and season to taste with salt and pepper; cover and set aside.

For the schnitzel, if the cutlets aren't thin enough, arrange them, side by side, between 2 sheets of plastic wrap. Use a meat pounder or your fist to tenderize and slightly flatten them. Place the flour, eggs, and bread-crumbs in 3 separate deep, wide plates.

cont'd

You can cook the schnitzel in one batch of 3, but it's more relaxed to cook them individually. In a large, heavy pan, heat 2 tablespoons of the butter and a generous splash of olive oil over high heat. Season 1 schnitzel on both sides with salt and pepper. Lightly dredge the schnitzel in the flour, then dip it in the egg and dredge it in the breadcrumbs, making sure it's evenly covered. Reduce the heat to medium-high, immediately place the schnitzel in the pan, and cook, turning once and reducing the heat, if necessary, for 1 to 1½ minutes per side or until golden and just cooked through. Transfer the schnitzel to a plate, then melt 1 tablespoon of butter in the pan and continue cooking the remaining schnitzel in the same way.

Divide the warm schnitzel and potato salad between plates and sprinkle both with a little pepper.

Polenta Lasagna Bolognese

SERVES 4

FOR THE BOLOGNESE SAUCE*

Olive oil, for sautéing

7 ounces (200 g) peeled carrots, cut in half lengthwise and thinly sliced

2 celery stalks, thinly sliced

1 medium onion, diced

1 large clove garlic

1 pound (450 g) ground beef

2 tablespoons tomato paste

2 cups (480 ml) full-bodied red wine, plus more as needed

14 ounces (400 g) canned whole peeled tomatoes, chopped

1 small bunch fresh thyme

1 small sprig fresh rosemary

2 bay leaves

Fine sea salt

Finely ground pepper

cont'd

Lasagna Bolognese made with thick layers of creamy polenta instead of pasta sheets and béchamel sauce feels almost light and is a fabulous take on this Italian classic. The shift from durum wheat to cornmeal doesn't decrease the cozy feeling—but it's less dense, less heavy, and won't force you to take a nap after lunch. First, you cook the polenta and then you let it cool in thick sheets. You can prepare the cornmeal and Bolognese the night before, a lazy endeavor once the sauce is simmering, and finish assembling it the next day. As I don't mind eating it twice in a row, I often indulge in half the recipe in the evening, when it's not yet assembled into a lasagna, and enjoy the other half, lusciously layered, for lunch the next day. It only takes fifteen minutes to reheat the lasagna in the oven and melt the Parmesan that is sandwiched in between the scrumptious layers.

For the Bolognese sauce, heat a generous splash of olive oil in a large, heavy pot over medium-high heat. Add the carrots, celery, onion, and whole garlic and sauté, stirring occasionally, for 5 minutes. Push the vegetables to the sides of the pot, then add a little more olive oil and the beef to the middle of the pot and cook, stirring to break up the meat, for a few minutes or until no more liquid comes out and the meat is browned. Add the tomato paste and cook, stirring, for 1 minute. Add the red wine and deglaze the pot, using a spatula to scrape any bits and pieces off the bottom. Bring to a boil and cook for 2 minutes. Add the tomatoes, thyme, rosemary, and bay leaves, then season with salt and pepper and bring to a boil again. Reduce the heat and simmer gently, uncovered and stirring occasionally, for 1 hour. The sauce should be thick and loose. If there's too much liquid left, turn up the heat and reduce the sauce; if it's too dry, add a little more wine. Remove and discard the garlic, thyme, rosemary, and bay leaves,

cont'd

1½ cups (360 ml) whole milk

1½ cups (360 ml) water,
plus more as needed

3 tablespoons olive oil

1½ teaspoons fine sea salt

1 cup plus 1 tablespoon
(180 g) fine polenta

2 ounces (60 g) Parmesan,
finely grated

Finely ground pepper

then season to taste with salt and pepper. Transfer the Bolognese sauce to a large, wide bowl and let it cool for at least 10 minutes.

Meanwhile, for the lasagna, in a medium pot, bring the milk, water, olive oil, and salt to a boil. Reduce the heat to the lowest setting, add the polenta, and whisk until combined. Cook the polenta for 10 minutes, stirring occasionally and adding a little more water when it starts to thicken; it should be thick, smooth, and creamy. Season to taste with salt, then immediately line a roughly 7 x 7-inch (18 x 18 cm) baking dish with plastic wrap and scrape half of the polenta into the lined dish; this will be the top layer of the lasagna and the plastic wrap will help transfer this layer on top of the bottom layer. Oil the bottom of another 7 x 7-inch (18 x 18 cm) baking dish and add the remaining polenta; this will be the bottom layer. Spread the polenta out evenly in both dishes, then let it cool for at least 10 minutes or until firm.

Preheat the oven to 400°F (200°C).

Scoop enough of the Bolognese sauce on top of the polenta in the oiled baking dish so that the Bolognese layer is roughly as thick as the polenta layer. Sprinkle with half of the Parmesan, then place the second polenta layer on top of the Bolognese sauce. Drizzle with a few spoonfuls of the Bolognese sauce, or use all of it, and sprinkle with half of the remaining Parmesan. Bake for about 15 minutes or until the lasagna is hot throughout and the cheese has melted. Sprinkle with the remaining Parmesan and a little pepper and serve immediately.

* You can use all the Bolognese sauce for the lasagna, but I only use about two-thirds. Keep leftover sauce, covered, in the fridge to use for pasta the next day or freeze it, in a container, for up to 3 months.

Coriander-Fennel Meatballs with Green Beans

SERVES 2

1 pound (450 g) ground beef

¼ cup (35 g) dry breadcrumbs

1 large egg

1 small onion, finely chopped

1 large clove garlic, crushed

1 tablespoon olive oil, plus more for cooking

1 tablespoon coriander seeds, crushed with a mortar and pestle

1 tablespoon fennel seeds, crushed with a mortar and pestle

1¾ teaspoons fine sea salt

1 teaspoon finely ground pepper

1 tablespoon unsalted butter

11 ounces (310 g) trimmed green beans

There's something very comforting about eating lunch right out of a pan—especially with a recipe that gives you reason enough to do so. Here, I use little beef meatballs, which are seasoned with lots of coriander and fennel seeds, tasting like a spiced-up coarse Italian sausage. Let the juicy meatballs settle into a hot pan and throw in blanched green beans to soak up all the beautiful buttery juices—you don't want to waste any of that fat and flavor. You'll end up eating this straight out of the pan, wiping up the last bits and pieces with chunks of soft white bread—and smiling happily. Although this recipe may seem involved for a midday meal, it only takes fifteen minutes to prepare.

In a large bowl, combine the ground beef, breadcrumbs, egg, onion, garlic, the 1 tablespoon of olive oil, coriander seeds, fennel seeds, salt, and pepper and mix with your hands until well combined. Form the mixture into 12 small meatballs and transfer to a plate.

In a large, heavy pan, heat the butter and a generous splash of olive oil over medium-high heat. Add the meatballs and cook, turning occasionally, for about 10 minutes or until golden brown and cooked through; reduce the heat if they brown too quickly.

While the meatballs are cooking, bring a large pot of salted water to a boil. Add the beans, reduce the heat, and blanch for 5 to 7 minutes or until tender. Drain the beans and briefly rinse with cold water, then transfer to a medium bowl and season with a little salt and pepper.

When the meatballs are done, add the beans to the pan, toss to coat with the buttery juices in the pan, and enjoy warm—or even cold.

Lamb Chops with Minty Mashed Peas

SERVES 1

5 ounces (140 g) fresh or frozen peas

About 20 fresh mint leaves, plus 8 thinly sliced leaves for serving

2 teaspoons freshly squeezed lemon juice

1½ tablespoons olive oil, plus more for cooking

Fine sea salt

Finely ground pepper

2 to 3 lamb chops (about 9 ounces / 250 g total)

Flaky sea salt

Coarsely ground pepper

If you feel a sudden craving for a meat-focused lunch, little lamb chops are a quick and hearty way to satisfy your longing. Just don't overcook them and you will be rewarded with tender, tasty chops, packed with a deep yet delicate meaty flavor. They only need to stay in the hot pan for a few minutes, so watch them closely. A dollop of minty puréed peas, bright green in taste and color, ensures the lamb chops don't lose their springy feeling. There's no need to peel fresh peas for this purée, just keep a bag in your freezer. It's handy and totally fine, especially when the peas end up in the blender anyway.

Bring a small pot of salted water to a boil and blanch the peas for 1 minute. Transfer to a colander, drain, and briefly rinse with cold water, then transfer to a blender or food processor. Add 15 of the mint leaves, the lemon juice, and the 1½ tablespoons of olive oil and purée briefly. If the mint flavor doesn't come through enough, add the remaining 5 mint leaves, then purée again and season to taste with fine sea salt and finely ground pepper. Transfer to a small bowl and set aside.

In a medium, heavy pan, heat a splash of olive oil over medium-high heat. Add the lamb chops and sear for 1½ to 2 minutes per side or until golden brown but still pink inside. Season to taste with flaky sea salt and coarsely ground pepper, then transfer to a plate and let rest for 3 minutes. Arrange the puréed peas next to the lamb chops, sprinkle with the sliced mint leaves, and enjoy warm.

Braised Chicken Breast with Tomato and Basil Oil

FOR THE BASIL OIL

1 large handful fresh basil
leaves, roughly chopped

1½ tablespoons olive oil

1 teaspoon freshly
squeezed lemon juice

FOR THE CHICKEN

Olive oil, for searing

1 medium boneless, skinless
chicken breast

Flaky sea salt

Coarsely ground pepper

6 fresh basil sprigs

½ cup (120 ml) dry white wine

1 large, ripe tomato, cut into
thick slices

Cooking chicken breast with fresh basil and white wine infuses the meat with the fragrant herb and allows it to become buttery tender in just ten minutes. There's only one rule: If the heat is too high, buttery and tender will turn into chewy and tough. So, keep the heat low and treat the meat gently. Dwelling blissfully in the summery mood, I slice a ripe, fleshy tomato and whisk together a quick basil oil to freshen up both the tomato and the braised chicken.

For the basil oil, whisk together the chopped basil, olive oil, and lemon juice in a small bowl and set aside.

For the chicken, heat a splash of olive oil in a medium saucepan over medium-high heat. Add the chicken breast and sear for 1 minute per side, then, while the chicken is still in the pan with the heat on, season generously with salt and pepper and arrange the basil sprigs underneath the chicken breast. Add the white wine and bring to a boil. As soon as it starts boiling, reduce the heat to a very low simmer, cover, and cook for about 10 minutes or until the chicken is tender and cooked through; mind that the heat stays low, or the meat will become tough.

Let the chicken rest for 5 minutes, then cut into thick slices and arrange on a plate. Place the tomato slices next to the chicken, season both the tomato and the chicken with a little salt and pepper, and drizzle with the basil oil. You can use cold leftover chicken for salads.

Mediterranean Meatloaf with Vegetables and Herbs

SERVES 6 TO 8

1½ cups (360 ml) whole milk

⅓ cup (45 g) dry breadcrumbs

2¼ pounds (1 kg) ground beef

5 ounces (140 g) zucchini, cut into small cubes

5 ounces (140 g) red bell pepper, cut into small cubes

5 ounces (140 g) yellow bell pepper, cut into small cubes

4 ounces (110 g) leek (white and green parts), cut in half lengthwise and cut into thin slices

2 large eggs

4 tablespoons finely chopped fresh flat-leaf parsley leaves

3 tablespoons fresh thyme leaves, plus 8 sprigs for the topping

1½ tablespoons finely chopped fresh rosemary needles

3½ teaspoons fine sea salt

Finely ground pepper

Zucchini, bell pepper, and leek might not come to mind when you think of meatloaf, but the vegetables help make it soft and juicy. The colorful little bites loosen up the texture and expand the hearty loaf's flavor with sweet and green tones. Lots of fresh herbs, including thyme, rosemary, and parsley, make it smell and taste like the Mediterranean. You can eat it warm, right after you pull it out of the oven, but a thick slice of cold meatloaf packed between two slices of bread is just as tempting. Getting comfy, sitting outside with this hearty sandwich on your lap, comes very close to lunch perfection. And this is exactly the reason why I never bother making a small meatloaf. It's so good that you have to share it with friends at your next weekend brunch or freeze it for sudden lunch cravings. Just cut the left-over baked loaf into thick slices and freeze them in single bags or containers. Utterly satisfying.

Preheat the oven to 350°F (180°C).

In a medium bowl, stir together the milk and breadcrumbs and let soak for 5 minutes.

In a large bowl, combine the ground beef, zucchini, red and yellow bell peppers, leek, eggs, parsley, thyme leaves, rosemary, salt, and a generous amount of pepper. Add the milk-breadcrumb mixture and mix together with your hands until well combined.

Transfer the meatloaf mixture to a baking dish and form into an 11 x 6-inch (28 x 15 cm) loaf. Arrange the thyme sprigs around and on top of the meatloaf and bake for about 1 hour and 20 minutes or until golden brown and completely cooked through. Serve warm or cold.

To freeze leftover meatloaf, cut the loaf into thick slices and freeze them in single bags or containers. There's no need to defrost; you can place the frozen slice into a baking dish and bake at 400°F (200°C) for about 25 minutes (depending on its thickness) or until completely hot throughout.

GRAINS

+

BAKES

Apricot Pancakes with Basil Sugar

MAKES 6 PANCAKES

FOR THE BASIL SUGAR

⅓ cup (70 g) granulated sugar

30 large fresh basil leaves

FOR THE PANCAKES

⅔ cup (90 g) all-purpose flour

¾ teaspoon baking powder

2 large eggs, separated

⅛ teaspoon fine sea salt

½ cup (120 ml) whole milk

2 to 3 tablespoons
unsalted butter

6 apricots, pitted and cut
into quarters

A few years ago, I ordered an apricot-basil crumble at a charming café in my Berlin neighborhood. I was skeptical but curious how the fragrant herb would perform in a sweet baked dish. It turns out, it was quite stunning. The basil pulled the whole thing in a more complex, grown-up direction. It works unbelievably well with stone fruit—especially apricots—where it can infuse their tart juicy pulp. For a dessert at a lunch party with friends, I would go for crêpes and apricot compote, but for an easy weekday treat, I make thick and fluffy pancakes. The egg white is beaten so that the apricots can nestle comfortably in the cloudlike batter. A handful of fresh basil leaves mixed with sugar and then generously sprinkled over the warm pancakes completes the feast.

For the basil sugar, briefly pulse the sugar and basil in a food processor or blender until fine; transfer to a small bowl and set aside.

For the pancakes, whisk together the flour and baking powder in a medium bowl.

In the bowl of a stand mixer fitted with the whisk attachment, whisk the egg whites and salt for 1 to 2 minutes or until stiff, then transfer to a bowl. Add the egg yolks and milk to the same bowl of the stand mixer and whisk for 1 minute, then add the flour mixture and mix until smooth. Using a large spoon, gently fold the egg whites into the batter.

In a large cast-iron pan or nonstick skillet, melt 2 teaspoons of the butter over medium-high heat. Making 2 to 3 pancakes at a time, pour in a ladle of the batter for each pancake and cook for 1 minute. Arrange 4 apricot quarters, skin-side up, on top of each pancake, gently pushing the fruit into the batter, and

cont'd

cook for 1 minute or until golden; reduce the heat if the pancakes brown too quickly. Flip the pancakes over, add 1 teaspoon of butter to the pan, and cook for 2 minutes; mind that the apricots don't burn. Flip the pancakes again and cook for 1 to 2 minutes or until baked through. Transfer to a large plate and generously sprinkle the warm pancakes with the basil sugar. Finish making pancakes with the remaining batter and apricots, adding a little more butter to the pan before each batch. Enjoy warm or cold.

Breton Buckwheat Galette with Gruyère and Egg

MAKES 8 GALETTES

6 tablespoons unsalted butter

2⅓ cups (550 ml) water

1½ cups (250 g) buckwheat flour

½ teaspoon fine sea salt

8 large eggs

5 ounces (140 g) Gruyère or Comté, finely grated

Coarsely ground pepper

A Breton galette is a hearty crêpe made with buckwheat flour, so no gluten will interfere with your crêpe-eating pleasure. The crêpe is often folded and filled with an aromatic cheese, such as Gruyère or Comté, or a creamy soft chèvre. When you crack an egg in the middle and sneak in a thin slice of ham, it's called galette complète. Although I usually don't say no to a slice of ham, in this case, I prefer to keep my crêpe ham-free. There's something particularly satisfying about this light and thin yet still fluffy buckwheat crêpe. I don't want to mess with it too much. The crispy sides are folded over the cheese, which is melting on top of the egg, with its white just set and its yolk still runny. It's simply perfect. Bénédict Berna brought this recipe into my life. The Berlin-based Frenchman taught me that the batter for a galette requires only buckwheat flour, water, a little melted butter, and salt—but no eggs.

Melt 2 tablespoons of the butter in a small saucepan, then take the pan off the heat and let the butter cool for a few minutes.

In a large bowl, whisk together the water, flour, and salt until smooth, then add the melted butter and whisk until combined. Cover the bowl and place in the fridge for at least 1 hour or up to 12 hours; briefly whisk the batter again before cooking the crêpes.

In a large cast-iron pan or nonstick skillet, melt 1 teaspoon of butter over medium-high heat. Pour in a ladle of the batter, tilting and turning the pan, so that the batter spreads evenly and thinly; it won't be as thin as a crêpe made with all-purpose flour, but if the batter is too thick and doesn't spread well, add a little more water. Cook the galette for 1 to 2 minutes or until golden on the bottom and just set on the top. Using a spatula, flip the galette, then let ½ teaspoon of

cont'd

butter melt underneath the crêpe. Reduce the heat to medium-low, then crack 1 egg in the middle of the galette and immediately sprinkle one-eighth of the cheese on top of the egg white. Using the ridge of a spatula, carve a square around the egg white, without cutting through the galette, then fold the 4 sides of the galette up and over the egg white, leaving the egg yolk uncovered. Keep the heat between medium-low and medium and cook the galette for about 7 minutes or until the egg white is just set, the yolk is still runny, and the cheese is melted; mind that the bottom of the galette doesn't burn. Transfer the galette to a plate, sprinkle with pepper, and enjoy immediately. You can let the galette sit for 10 to 15 minutes, so you can continue cooking the remaining galettes in the same way, but make sure it doesn't cool completely; it tastes best when the egg yolk is still warm.

Dutch Baby with Taleggio and Pear

SERVES 2 TO 4

½ cup (120 ml) whole milk

2 large eggs

1 cup (130 g) all-purpose flour, sifted

⅛ teaspoon fine sea salt

⅓ cup plus 1 tablespoon (90 g) unsalted butter

2 ounces (60 g) Taleggio, cut into small cubes

½ firm pear, cored and cut into thin wedges

Coarsely ground pepper

Marta Greber of the food blog *What Should I Eat for Breakfast Today?* introduced me to the famous Dutch baby in her Berlin kitchen many, many years ago. As she pulled the hot skillet out of the oven, I was immediately smitten with the golden pancake that resembled a cloud that wouldn't stop rising. It's such a dramatic dish, although it's basically just a pancake baked in the oven in a puddle of sizzling butter. It's also quick and simple and by varying the toppings, a Dutch baby can wear many hats. Marta went for sweet, adding chocolate and berries. I love the combination of melted Taleggio and crisp pear, which feels more like an adult Dutch baby. Whatever finish you're going for, a Dutch baby is always a stunner on a weekend brunch table and a spectacular surprise at lunchtime during the week.

Preheat the oven to 425°F (220°C).

In a large bowl, whisk together the milk and eggs, then add the flour and salt and whisk for 1 minute or until smooth. Let the batter sit for about 10 minutes.

When the oven is hot, add the butter to a 10-inch (25 cm) ovenproof skillet, then place the skillet on the bottom rack of the oven. When the butter has melted completely, wait for 1 minute, then carefully and slowly pour the batter in the middle of the pan into the melted butter and quickly close the oven door. Bake the Dutch baby for about 12 minutes or until golden and risen; don't open the door while it's baking. Carefully remove the skillet from the oven and place on a trivet. Arrange the Taleggio and pear in the middle of the hot Dutch baby, sprinkle with a little pepper, and enjoy immediately.

German Cinnamon-Apple Pancake

MAKES 2 PANCAKES

1 cup (240 ml) whole milk

3 large eggs

2 tablespoons granulated sugar, plus 1 tablespoon for serving

⅛ teaspoon fine sea salt

1 cup (130 g) all-purpose flour, sifted

¼ teaspoon ground cinnamon, plus ¼ teaspoon for serving

3 tablespoons unsalted butter

2 medium, tart baking apples, cored and cut into round slices

Apple pancakes are a fond childhood memory for many people. In Germany, they are a kids' lunch staple—I still remember my mother cooking them for my sister and me. While American-style pancakes tend to be small and fluffy, German-style pancakes are large, flat, dense, and a bit silky like a flan. The egg white isn't beaten, so the texture is similar to that of crêpes, just thicker. Covering a pancake with apple slices is the classic approach, but you can top it with almost any fruit that isn't too juicy or fragile. Plums and apricots are a scrumptious alternative and, like apples, also benefit from a generous sprinkle of cinnamon sugar.

In the bowl of a stand mixer fitted with the whisk attachment, whisk together the milk, eggs, the 2 tablespoons of sugar, and the salt. Add the flour and ¼ teaspoon of cinnamon and whisk until smooth. Let the batter sit for about 10 minutes.

In a small bowl, combine the remaining 1 tablespoon of sugar and the remaining ¼ teaspoon of cinnamon and set aside.

In a 10-inch (25 cm) cast-iron pan or nonstick skillet, melt 1 tablespoon of the butter over medium-high heat. Pour half the batter into the pan and arrange half the apple slices, side by side, on top. Cook the pancake, adjusting the heat as necessary, for about 3 minutes or until golden on the bottom and just set on the top. Quickly flip the pancake onto a large lid, then add ½ tablespoon of butter to the pan, let the pancake slide off the lid into the pan, and cook for 2 to 3 minutes or until the bottom is golden brown. Flip the pancake onto a large plate and sprinkle with half of the cinnamon sugar. Cook the second pancake in the same way, melting butter in the pan before adding the batter. Sprinkle with the remaining cinnamon sugar and enjoy warm or cold.

Crêpes with Lemon and Cinnamon

MAKES 8 CRÊPES

1¼ cups (300 ml) whole milk

2 large eggs

1 cup (130 g) all-purpose flour, sifted

2 tablespoons granulated sugar, plus 2 tablespoons for the topping

⅛ teaspoon fine sea salt

½ teaspoon ground cinnamon

4 teaspoons unsalted butter

2 to 3 large lemons, cut in half

I had my first crêpe au citron during a mother-daughter weekend trip to Le Touquet, a picturesque seaside town in northern France. When I saw the baker squeeze more than a tablespoon of lemon juice onto my paper-thin pancake, I was baffled, but only until I took the first bite. Lemon quickly became my favorite crêpe topping—that is, until I discovered that adding cinnamon sugar to the tart juices raises the crêpe game to new heights.

In the bowl of a stand mixer fitted with the whisk attachment, whisk together the milk, eggs, flour, 2 tablespoons of sugar, and the salt until smooth. Let the batter sit for about 10 minutes.

In a small bowl, whisk together the remaining 2 tablespoons of sugar and the cinnamon.

In a large cast-iron pan or nonstick skillet, melt ½ teaspoon of the butter over medium-high heat. Pour in a ladle of the batter, tilting and turning the pan, so that the batter spreads evenly and very thinly. Cook the crêpe, flipping once, for 30 to 60 seconds per side or until golden, then transfer to a large plate. Sprinkle with a little of the cinnamon sugar and drizzle generously with freshly squeezed lemon juice. Fold the crêpe in half twice so it forms a triangle, then transfer to another plate and cover to keep warm. Finish making crêpes with the remaining batter, adding a little more butter to the pan between crêpes and adjusting the heat as necessary. Immediately sprinkle each crêpe with cinnamon sugar and drizzle with lemon juice, then fold into triangles.

Divide the warm crêpes among plates and add more cinnamon sugar and lemon juice to taste. The crêpes taste best when they are warm, but you can keep them, covered, in the fridge for up to 1 day.

Tahini Oats with Roasted Rhubarb

SERVES 1

FOR THE TOPPING

4 ounces (110 g) trimmed rhubarb, cut into long, slender pieces

1 tablespoon olive oil

Fine sea salt

2 to 3 tablespoons goat milk yogurt (or Greek yogurt)

6 small fresh basil leaves

FOR THE OATS

⅓ cup (40 g) rolled oats

½ to ¾ cup (120 to 180 ml) water

1 to 1½ teaspoons light tahini

1 teaspoon honey

Fine sea salt

The first dish I ever prepared for myself as a child—and keep preparing to this day—was oatmeal. When I started this tradition, at about five years old, I sprinkled plain rolled oats with unsweetened Dutch cocoa powder and sugar and poured cold milk over it. I ate it every day. Although the bowl I served my oats in never changed, times changed, I changed, and so the recipe changed. These days, I often have warm oats for lunch, with tahini, honey, and sea salt and crown it with goat milk yogurt and roasted rhubarb. Sometimes, I just sprinkle my oats with fresh berries, fruit compote, or thickly sliced banana. And when I'm feeling really adventurous, I opt for unusual savory additions. It may sound weird, but the Roasted Brussels Sprouts with Orange and Cinnamon (page 90) mingles remarkably smoothly with creamy oats. I dedicate this recipe to my father, who, thanks to tahini and exciting toppings, could be convinced that oatmeal isn't that bad after all.

Preheat the oven to 400°F (200°C).

For the topping, in a medium baking dish, toss the rhubarb and olive oil, season with a little salt, and roast for about 20 minutes or until soft; you can use the rhubarb warm or cold.

Meanwhile, for the oats, combine the rolled oats, ½ cup (120 ml) of water, 1 teaspoon of tahini, the honey, and ⅛ teaspoon of salt in a medium saucepan and bring to a boil, stirring constantly. Take the saucepan off the heat and continue stirring vigorously for 10 seconds to fluff it up; add a little more water if the oats are too thick. Season to taste with additional tahini and salt, then transfer the porridge to a bowl. Plop the yogurt on top of the warm porridge and arrange the rhubarb on top. Sprinkle with the basil and enjoy.

Parsnip and Pear Tart with Gorgonzola and Thyme

SERVES 3 TO 4

FOR THE PASTRY

2 cups (260 g) all-purpose flour

1 teaspoon fine sea salt

½ cup plus 1 tablespoon (130 g) unsalted butter, cold

1 large egg

FOR THE TOPPING

8 ounces (225 g) trimmed parsnips, rinsed and cut into thin wedges

3 tablespoons olive oil

1 tablespoon honey

Fine sea salt

1 large, firm pear, cored and cut into wedges

4 ounces (110 g) Gorgonzola, cut into cubes

15 fresh small thyme sprigs

Coarsely ground pepper

Parsnip, pear, and blue cheese are a perfect autumn trio, especially when they meet in a buttery tart. You could use Roquefort or Stilton, but I prefer the sweetness of Gorgonzola. It melts so smoothly into the parsnip and pear. To save time, you can opt for a store-bought crust, or prepare it in advance and keep it in the fridge or freezer. A slice of cold leftover tart with a green salad at noon makes the most satisfying and nourishing lunch. And when you pull the tart out of the oven the night before, still fragrant and warm, it's the coziest dinner I can think of.

For the pastry, combine the flour and salt in the bowl of a stand mixer fitted with the paddle attachment. Add the butter and use a knife to cut it into the flour until there are just small pieces left. Quickly rub the butter into the flour with your fingers until combined. Add the egg and mix on low just until the dough comes together. Form the dough into a thick disc, wrap it in plastic wrap, and freeze for 10 minutes.

For the topping, bring a medium pot of salted water to a boil and blanch the parsnip wedges for 4 to 5 minutes or until al dente. Drain gently, minding that the wedges stay in one piece, then briefly rinse with cold water and let them dry for a few minutes.

In a medium pot, whisk together the olive oil and honey over medium heat, then add the parsnips and gently toss until evenly coated. Season with a little salt and remove from the heat.

Preheat the oven to 400°F (200°C).

On a work surface, place the dough between 2 sheets of plastic wrap and use a rolling pin to roll out into a disc, large enough to line the bottom and sides of a 12-inch (30 cm) quiche dish. Fit the dough into the

cont'd

quiche dish, pushing it into the dish, especially along the edges. Let the dough hang over the rim or trim with a knife. Use a fork to prick the dough all over. Bake for about 15 minutes or until golden. If the dough bubbles up, push it down with a fork.

Take the quiche dish out of the oven. Arrange the parsnip and pear wedges, alternating and like rays, in a circle on top of the prebaked pastry and drizzle with any of the honey-olive oil mixture that's left in the pot. Sprinkle with the Gorgonzola and thyme sprigs and bake for 19 to 22 minutes or until the pastry is golden and crispy and the cheese has melted. Let the tart cool for 10 minutes, then sprinkle with some pepper and enjoy warm or cold.

Fennel and Alpine Cheese Quiche

SERVES 3 TO 4

FOR THE PASTRY

2 cups (260 g) all-purpose flour

1 teaspoon fine sea salt

½ cup plus 1 tablespoon (130 g) unsalted butter, cold

1 large egg

FOR THE FILLING

Olive oil, for sautéing

1 (14-ounce / 400 g) fennel bulb, cut in half lengthwise, cored, and thinly sliced lengthwise

Fine sea salt

Finely ground pepper

3 large eggs

½ cup (120 ml) heavy cream

½ cup (120 g) sour cream or crème fraîche

Nutmeg, preferably freshly grated

3 ounces (85 g) Raclette, Gruyère, Appenzeller, or any aromatic cheese that melts well, coarsely grated

I love a good quiche. For me, the pastry needs to be thin and flaky, buttery but light, and the filling shouldn't be too high. It's about finding the right ratio of base to filling, so that the quiche is packed with potent flavors yet still allows enough space for the short-crust pastry to shine through. My basic quiche recipe has never changed—it's as reliable as a good old friend—but the fillings vary. Focusing on the seasons and featuring different produce keeps it exciting and leads to the most satisfying results. Fennel offers subtle sweetness and pairs so well with an aromatic hard Alpine cheese, such as Raclette or Gruyère, which keeps the quiche hearty and smoothly melts into the silky egg-cream filing.

For the pastry, combine the flour and salt in the bowl of a stand mixer fitted with the paddle attachment. Add the butter and use a knife to cut it into the flour until there are just small pieces left. Quickly rub the butter into the flour with your fingers until combined. Add the egg and mix on low just until the dough comes together. Form the dough into a thick disc, wrap it in plastic wrap, and freeze for 10 minutes.

Preheat the oven to 400°F (200°C).

For the filling, heat a splash of olive oil in a large, heavy pan over medium-high heat. Add the fennel and sauté, stirring occasionally, for 7 minutes or until golden and al dente. Season to taste with salt and pepper and let it cool for at least 10 minutes.

On a work surface, place the dough between 2 sheets of plastic wrap and use a rolling pin to roll out into an oval, large enough to line the bottom and sides of an oval-shaped 8 x 12-inch (20 x 30 cm) baking dish. Fit the dough into the baking dish, pushing it into the

cont'd

dish, especially along the edges. Use a fork to prick the dough all over. Bake for 15 minutes or until golden. If the dough bubbles up, push it down with a fork. Take the quiche dish out of the oven and reduce the heat to 350°F (180°C).

In a medium bowl, whisk together the eggs, heavy cream, sour cream, ¾ teaspoon of salt, and generous amounts of pepper and nutmeg.

Arrange the fennel on top of the prebaked pastry, layer the cheese on top, and pour the egg mixture over the fennel and cheese. Bake for about 35 minutes or until the top is golden and firm and the pastry is crispy. Let the quiche cool for at least 10 minutes and enjoy warm or cold.

Peach Tart with Stilton and Thyme

SERVES 3 TO 4

FOR THE PASTRY

2 cups (260 g) all-purpose flour

1 teaspoon fine sea salt

½ cup plus 1 tablespoon (130 g) unsalted butter, cold

1 large egg

FOR THE TOPPING

3 large white doughnut peaches, cut in half lengthwise

2 large yellow peaches, cut into quarters

2½ tablespoons olive oil

3 ounces (85 g) Stilton or Roquefort, crumbled

15 fresh small thyme sprigs, plus 1 tablespoon thyme leaves

Flaky sea salt

Coarsely ground pepper

Bake your peach tart in the evening and take it with you to work the next day. At noon, go outside and sit down in a park, and when you munch on the first mouthful, close your eyes. Buttery pastry, chunky peaches, Stilton, and thyme, all in one bite, taste like a summer holiday memory turned into food. The sweet, fruity juices and salty cheese can almost compete with a blissful day at the beach.

Follow the recipe for the pastry (page 259) and freeze for 10 minutes.

Preheat the oven to 400°F (200°C).

On a work surface, place the dough between 2 sheets of plastic wrap and use a rolling pin to roll out into a disc, large enough to line the bottom and sides of a 10 to 12-inch (25.5 to 30 cm) quiche dish; a smaller quiche dish makes a thicker pastry base, which is nice for the peaches. Fit the dough into the quiche dish, pushing it into the dish, especially along the edges. Use a fork to prick the dough all over. Bake for about 15 minutes or until golden. If the dough bubbles up, push it down with a fork.

For the topping, arrange the peaches in circles on top of the prebaked pastry; for the middle of the tart, cut 2 yellow peach quarters in half again and arrange in a small circle. Drizzle with the olive oil, then sprinkle with the Stilton, thyme sprigs, and a little flaky sea salt. Bake for about 23 minutes or until the pastry is golden and crispy and the cheese is melted. Take the tart out of the oven, then immediately sprinkle with the thyme leaves and a little pepper. Let the tart cool for at least 15 minutes. Enjoy warm or cold.

Grape Tart with Chèvre and Rosemary

SERVES 3 TO 4

FOR THE PASTRY

2 cups (260 g) all-purpose flour

1 teaspoon fine sea salt

½ cup plus 1 tablespoon (130 g) unsalted butter, cold

1 large egg

FOR THE TOPPING

17 ounces (480 g) seedless red grapes

1 tablespoon olive oil

Flaky sea salt

4 ounces (110 g) chèvre or Camembert, cut into slices

1 tablespoon finely chopped fresh rosemary needles

Coarsely ground pepper

1 tablespoon honey

This savory tart smells and tastes like a late summer afternoon in the south of France. The grapes' plump skins are popping and bursting in the heat, while their juices merge with the creamy chèvre melting on top. You could also use Camembert, which is sharper and more mature than chèvre and would be a bit more dominant. I like to drizzle the baked tart with a little honey to enhance its natural sweetness without making it too sweet. I always use homemade short-crust pastry, which you can also freeze for weeks or keep in the fridge for forty-eight hours, but feel free to use store-bought crust, or even puff pastry. Just adjust the baking time.

Follow the recipe for the pastry (page 259) and freeze for 10 minutes.

Preheat the oven to 400°F (200°C).

On a work surface, place the dough between 2 sheets of plastic wrap and use a rolling pin to roll out into an oval, large enough to line the bottom and sides of an oval-shaped 8 x 12-inch (20 x 30 cm) baking dish. Fit the dough into the baking dish, pushing it into the dish, especially along the edges. Use a fork to prick the dough all over. Bake for about 15 minutes or until golden. If the dough bubbles up, push it down with a fork.

For the topping, toss the grapes with the olive oil, then spread on top of the prebaked pastry. Sprinkle with a little flaky sea salt and arrange the chèvre on top. Bake for 20 to 23 minutes or until the pastry is golden and crispy and the grapes start to soften; the grapes might burst, which is fine. Take the tart out of the oven and immediately sprinkle with the rosemary and a little pepper. In a small saucepan, melt the honey, then drizzle over the warm grapes. Let the tart cool for at least 15 minutes. Keep a piece for the next day, it's just as nice cold.

The Best Quiche with Leek, Tomatoes, and Thyme

SERVES 3 TO 4

FOR THE PASTRY

2 cups (260 g) all-purpose flour

1 teaspoon fine sea salt

½ cup plus 1 tablespoon (130 g) unsalted butter, cold

1 large egg

FOR THE FILLING

4 large eggs

⅔ cup (160 g) sour cream or crème fraîche

½ cup (120 ml) heavy cream

3 tablespoons fresh thyme leaves, plus 6 small sprigs for the topping

1¼ teaspoons fine sea salt

Finely ground pepper

Nutmeg, preferably freshly grated

6 ounces (170 g) leek (white and green parts), thickly sliced

12 grape or cherry tomatoes, cut in half lengthwise

This is the first quiche recipe I ever came up with many years ago, and it sparked a lifelong love for this frugal but versatile dish. Pairing leek and tomato for the filling may sound unspectacular, but add a generous amount of fresh thyme and the magic starts to happen. It's a proper picnic quiche, spreading its irresistible picnic vibes even if you're just sitting inside at your desk. Enjoy it warm or cold, during your lunch break or shared with friends. Placing a warm quiche in the middle of the table at dinnertime and chatting long into the night over glasses of red wine has created some of my dearest memories. I often bake this quiche in the evening and feel so spoiled when I can slip a slice of it onto my plate at noon.

Follow the recipe for the pastry (page 259) and freeze for 10 minutes.

Preheat the oven to 400°F (200°C).

On a work surface, place the dough between 2 sheets of plastic wrap and use a rolling pin to roll out into a disc, large enough to line the bottom and sides of a 12-inch (30 cm) quiche dish. Fit the dough into the quiche dish, pushing it into the dish, especially along the edges. Let the dough hang over the rim or trim with a knife. Use a fork to prick the dough all over. Bake for 15 minutes or until golden. If the dough bubbles up, push it down with a fork. Take the quiche dish out of the oven and reduce the heat to 350°F (180°C).

For the filling, whisk together the eggs, sour cream, heavy cream, thyme leaves, salt, and generous amounts of pepper and nutmeg in a medium bowl.

Arrange the leek and tomatoes, cut-side up, on top of the prebaked pastry and pour the egg mixture over the vegetables. Sprinkle the thyme sprigs on top and bake for 50 to 55 minutes or until the top is golden and firm and the pastry is crispy. Let the quiche cool for at least 10 minutes. Enjoy warm or cold.

Acknowledgments

To all my friends, I want to thank you for being the solid rocks you are in my life. You make the daily ride more fun and inspire me to dive into a book like *Noon*—and to trust that it will all work out in the end. You make me braver, and I hope that I do the same for you.

Gabi, *Noon* wouldn't exist without you. Our friendship and our conversations are woven into every single page of this book. Our paths crossed when the world turned upside down; I definitely turned with it, and you helped me find orientation again. I will be forever thankful that we found each other.

Anne, you make me feel the ground again when I've been swept off my feet. Thank you for our friendship, for the ongoing creativity and inspiration that keeps flowing from your life into mine, but especially for the most beautiful gift you brought into this world, your daughter, Toni.

Toni, your parents couldn't have packed more joy, love, and beauty into one person. You are the sparkling sprinkles in my life, your hugs change everything, and there's no one I'd rather share my porridge—and bracelets—with. Thank you for being who you are.

Laurel, your wise words and tender smile will always guide me in the right direction. Thank you for being the best friend, for knowing when and how to challenge me but also when I need a safe spot to rest—and for always offering that spot. Having you—and your bakery and wine bar—in Berlin is one of the best things that could happen to me, and to this city.

My Mama, no one feeds me with more curiosity and inspiration when it comes to food than you. Cooking, eating, traveling, and discussing recipes with you is a precious gift. Being your daughter makes me who I am, as a cook and as a person, and I couldn't be happier about it.

Holly, *Noon* is our third book together. Be it destiny, the universe—I don't care—there's no other person I'd rather have at my side as an editor and friend. You were the first to believe in me as an author and taught me to believe in myself. Whenever I get lost on this journey, I know that you're there. You've been my compass from day one. Thank you.

My Berlin parents, Ursula and Uwe, thank you for endless conversations and dinners, for your trust and patience. You are the reason I first came to this city, and you are one of the reasons why I stayed. Thank you, Tobias, for thirty-three years of friendship, for debating unanswerable questions at any time. Judith, your talent to challenge and soothe my mind at the same time keeps leading to the best adventures; thank you. Sandra, our daily laughs and chats at your shop are bliss. No one makes shopping for vegetables more fun than you. Thank you, Sandy, for always being up to discuss profound and trivial issues of life, even at seven in the morning.

Everyone at Chronicle who's been involved in this adventure, thank you for believing in *Noon* and for trusting that we would turn it into the wonderful book that it became. Lauren Salkeld, thank you for shaping my words, and Jen Endom, for polishing my photographs. Thank you, Stefanie Hering—your beautiful plates brighten up any recipe.

Ada, Gabi, Seán, and Viktoria, thank you for daily cappuccinos and chats, and for testing the recipes for *Noon*. Bringing the food from this book to the café around noon and sharing it with you made this book production the most joyful I've ever had.

To the readers of my books and my blog, *eat in my kitchen*, thank you for cooking my recipes for so many years and for encouraging me to always come up with new ideas—and new cookbooks.

Index

Chronicle Books publishes distinctive books and gifts. From award-winning children's titles, bestselling cookbooks, and eclectic pop culture to acclaimed works of art and design, stationery, and journals, we craft publishing that's instantly recognizable for its spirit and creativity. Enjoy our publishing and become part of our community at www.chroniclebooks.com.